A NOBLE FUNCTION

HOW U-HAUL® MOVED AMERICA

LUKE KRUEGER

BARRICADE BOOKS

FORT LEE, NJ

Published by Barricade Books Inc.
185 Bridge Plaza North
Suite 308-A
Fort Lee, NJ 07024

www.barricadebooks.com

Library of Congress Cataloging-in-Publication Data

Krueger, Luke.
A noble function : how U-Haul moved America/Luke Krueger.
p. cm.
Includes bibliographical references and index.

ISBN-13: 978-1-56980-329-5 (hbk. : alk. paper)
ISBN-10: 1-56980-329-3 (hbk. : alk. paper)

1. U-Haul International—History. 2. Storage and moving trade—United States—History—
20th century. 3. Moving, Household—United States—History—20th century. I. Title.

HF5488.U4K78 2007
388.3'243—dc22

2007001210

First Printing
Manufactured in the United States of America

CONTENTS

CONTENTS

ACKNOWLEDGMENTS

THIS BOOK WOULD not have been possible without the help of many people who offered their time and service. I am exceptionally grateful to the following U-Haul System members (employees) who were gracious hosts to this unknown writer who contacted them out of the blue. They welcomed me into their homes, fed me and, most importantly, shared their memories with me in an effort to retell the story of U-Haul and its growth from an idea into an industry. Their interviews were invaluable. (Note: Rental Company Managers [RCMs] became Rental Company Presidents [RCPs] in 1961.)

Jerry Ayres—Former head of Repair Accounting at ARCOA.

William E. "Hap" Carty—U-Haul co-founder Anna Mary Carty's younger brother, built the first trailers with co-founder L.S. "Sam" Shoen, set up Boston Trailer Manufacturing. Was in charge of the Northeast rental companies. Later was president of U-Haul International. Served on various Company boards of directors since 1950. Now currently on the AMERCO and U-Haul Boards of Directors.

Martin Carty—Anna Mary's youngest brother, helped paint the first trailers, the best source for an eyewitness account of Anna Mary and Sam's time on the Carty Ranch.

Pat Crahan—Former RCP of Oklahoma and Arkansas. Currently the director of Government Relations.

Elaine DeShong—Formerly in charge of Customer Relations. Husband Harry DeShong Sr. ran Arizona and Nevada rental company.

Charles Dreisbach—First ARCOA office manager; left in 1951 to become a priest.

Logan Frank—Former RCM of Florida, later RCM of Arizona and Nevada, an innovator in marketing U-Haul products. With 50 years of service in the System, he is currently the assistant to President and CEO Joe Shoen.

Ron Frank—Former area field manager (AFM) and RCM. He is now the executive vice president of U-Haul.

Dale Green—Worked at Willow Grove and as an AFM in Southern California.

Ron Green—Built trailers in Portland, Boston and Willow Grove. He also worked in the Research and Development Department.

Jacque Hedwall—Office worker in ARCOA since 1957; a remarkable resource for the basic history of U-Haul, she was an invaluable tutor in helping me better understand how the System worked.

Henry Kelly—Worked in Willow Grove and Steiner Body, and headed up the Holbrook and Novi manufacturing plants. Currently the vice president of Industrial Relations.

Bert Layman—Cousin of L.S. Shoen, a childhood friend and confidant.

Ann Lorentz—Wife of Jack Lorentz, who provided insights and anecdotes regarding her husband, Anna Mary Shoen and the life of a U-Haul wife.

Frank Lyons—Brother-in-law of Hap Carty and Anna Mary Carty Shoen; headed up Warrington Equipment Manufacturing. Now on the AMERCO Board of Directors.

Ray Robbins—First marketing director and early cartoonist. Robbins did three stints with U-Haul. He left to serve in the military and attend art school.

Theo Schader—Secretary to L.S. Shoen.

Phil Schnee—Built trailers in Boston; was an RCM. Currently, he is in charge of truck sales for the Idaho company.

Vivian Shaw—Headed up data-entry work for ARCOA offices in Portland.

Jim Shaw—Later Vivian's husband, he started as an AFM in Oakland before taking over the Southern California rental company, where he oversaw over 1,000 dealers.

Don Shivers—Early fleet owner. Built trailers in Portland, Boston, and Denver. Cousin to Anna Mary and Hap. Retired at 35 with his earnings as a fleet owner.

Ralph Shivers Jr.—Created the Traffic Department. One of the early AFMs and an RCM. Later, president of U-Haul International. He is Don's older brother. His brother Ken worked in the System, as did their parents.

Suzanne Anderson Shoen—Second wife of L.S. "Sam" Shoen. She had five children with him and raised the other six from his previous marriage to Anna Mary Carty Shoen.

Jim Simer—An AFM for Western Oregon. Simer later ran the Portland Repair Shop.

Duane Swanson—Longtime Director of Marketing, Swanson oversaw the color change, logo change and design of many U-Haul products.

Dale Webber—One of the first AFMs, he ran the shop in Oakland before eventually moving to the Midwest to run the manufacturing plant in Des Moines, and later running the Rental Company of Indiana.

Richard Wrublik—Director of Finance for ARCOA, he successfully implemented the Fleet Owner Program and secured U-Haul its first $2 million line of credit.

John Zuransky—Lifelong System member who has worked at Boston Trailer Manufacturing since 1958.

Further research came from interviews collected in 1988 by other System members. Some of these interviews were done with people who are now deceased. It is fortunate that we have their stories from these interviews. The '88 interviews were with: Dale Green, Vin Kiley (U-Haul Company of New England office manager, area field manager and special-projects manager for Hap Carty), Pat Crahan, Richard Wrublik, Tom O'Donnell (office manager of ARCOA until 1967), Helen Shoen (wife of Kermit Shoen, a System member and cousin to L.S.), Jim Simer,

Mike Morelli (longtime dealer in Portland, Oregon) and Jim and Vivian Shaw.

In general, the quotes attributed to those who witnessed the first twenty years were taken either from their 1988 interview or their 2005 interview. Specific attribution from the transcripts of the 1988 interviews can be found toward the back of the book in the endnotes. Quotes from the 2005 interviews do not receive footnotes.

Quotes attributed to L. S. "Sam" Shoen came primarily from *You and Me,* a book he penned, published by AMERCO in 1980 (ghost written by Gene McKinney).

Additional thanks must be given to Sister Carole Strawn of Marylhurst College, who provided me with material from Anna Mary's yearbooks compiled during her time at Marylhurst. Also, I want to thank James R. Forman, senior master technician for Ford Motor Company, who was consulted in order for me to better grasp automotive terms and developments in engineering.

Writing is a lonely task. Authors need a collaborator to let them know their journey is not a solitary endeavor. I want to thank Tom Prefling, Director of Communications, for assisting me and overseeing this project. His patience and timely encouragement made this project that much more enjoyable. A *very* special thanks goes to his wonderful staff, Meg Maher, Corporate Librarian and Alan Weinstein, Business Publications Specialist. They provided me with stacks of archival research, edited my drafts and gave crucial feedback regarding the story's narrative. If any credit for the success of this book should be given, it is to Meg, Alan and Tom.

Finally, I want to thank my family: my sisters, Marla and Kristi, and my parents, Bill and Marlene Krueger, who, no matter how excited I was to be writing this book, always exceeded my exuberance. Alette Noelani Valencia listened to drafts, listened to endless U-Haul stories (working on the material), and put up with constant isolation while I worked alone in my office.

Thank you all for your time and patience.

PREFACE

"We were all delighted, we all realized we were leaving confusion and nonsense behind and performing our one and noble function of the time, move."
                    —JACK KEROUAC, *On the Road*, 1957

WHEN I RECEIVED the offer to write about the first twenty years of U-Haul, Jon Odom, a friend of mine asked, "What do you know about U-Haul?" Later he asked, "Who are you writing it for?" The first question was easy to answer. What I knew about U-Haul was only that I once had rented a U-Haul truck to move from one apartment to another. The second question raised the critical dilemma of trying to frame the purpose of the book and my responsibility as a writer. In researching this book, however, I discovered that these two questions were the central principles of this project.

It is an interesting and delicate position to be put in, that of being hired by a company to write about it from an outsider's perspective. While I was sure many people at U-Haul were proud of the time and effort they had spent building the company, I did not want to write a maudlin piece that came across as sentimental cheerleading. What I knew in my initial meetings with Joe Shoen, President and CEO of U-Haul, and Tom Prefling, Director of Communications for U-Haul, was that the company's birth was a compelling story of resourcefulness and evolution. It would require immense blocks of time spent researching American history. To tell it would demand hours of interviews.

Ultimately, here's what the research revealed: it was a good story, seamlessly woven into the fabric of American history.

There is a balancing act to this writing as well. L.S. "Sam" Shoen is without a doubt the preeminent character in this narrative, but I think he would be quick to point out that his is not the only story. Sam enjoyed delegating work to other people and watching them rise to the challenge. He was known to drop people off and say, "I need a factory built here." And off he went to his next endeavor. He reveled in their success as well as his own.

During his interviews, Hap Carty, Sam's brother-in-law and U-Haul pioneer, hated to name specific people because he feared he would forget someone. Throughout our interviews he continually drove home the point that this story is about the people who made the company.

U-Haul grew and prospered because of a cast of characters who created departments, marketing strategies and products without precedent. They were inventive because they were pioneering a new industry.

It was in meeting these people that I felt reassured that this book would not be cheerleading. Meeting with people like Hap Carty, Logan Frank, Dick Wrublik, Jacque Hedwall, Jim Simer and the multitude of other System members from whom you will hear in this book, made me realize I was envious of how proud they were of those first twenty years. It is hard to imagine now, but in listening to them recall those years, it became apparent just how precarious a proposition U-Haul was. So when a certain sparkle came into their eyes and they spoke about how they "bleed orange" or lauded Sam, it was clear why: nearly every person interviewed never believed, in those early years, that U-Haul would be as common a household name as Kleenex is to tissues or Coke is to soft drinks—not even Sam. Yet today, when people rent a trailer or truck, regardless of the rental company, they say they are "renting a U-Haul."

John Zuransky, a long-time System member with Boston Trailer Manufacturing, tells the story of a time when Sam visited Boston Trailer Manufacturing Co. in the '70s and suddenly began laughing uncontrollably. When Zuransky asked Sam why he was laughing, Sam said he figured that if U-Haul lasted twenty years he would be happy. He never saw U-Haul lasting thirty-five, let alone sixty years. Sam's choice of years was an odd coincidence, considering that this book covers the first twenty, and within those twenty years, the growth of U-Haul was meteoric because of its product, its people and the time it came onto the scene in American history.

U-Haul was born at the right time. When Sam and Anna Mary Carty Shoen began renting trailers in 1945, Americans wanted to go, go, go! Or as Ron Frank said, "As the song goes, you can't send the boy back to the farm when he's been to Paris." The fact that Americans were on the move is well documented in various books on U.S. history. Oddly, though, while these books talk of housing, jobs and ways to spend disposable income, they (the books) never describe how Americans of that time moved to locations where limitless opportunity awaited them. U-Haul was born at a time of unbridled growth. It was a time when service stations were ports of entry for families moving into a new community. America had suffered through the Great Depression in the '30s; a world war in the '40s; the Baby Boom was underway; families needed a cheap and effective method for moving their fledgling kin. Van-line movers were available to those with money but not to the average American. So it is logical that trailers, a relatively simple product to construct, became the Conestoga wagon of postwar America.

Thus we return to my friend's initial questions: What did I know about U-Haul? Who was the book for? What I know about U-Haul is what you will read in this book, and I promise it will not be simplistic or maudlin. The people who built this company truly "bleed orange," and I can only hope to convey the enthusiasm I saw when they were asked to talk about U-Haul. I am writing this book in part for them because it is a story worth telling and one that no one else has told. I am also writing this book for the people who entered the System in the later years, long after 1964 and in the present day, so the tradition and essence of what propelled the company from an idea to an industry is not lost. In so doing, I hope to preserve the purpose and vision of the people who helped build the company. It's a great story.

AN IDEA
(1945–1951)

1

THE RELUCTANT BUSINESSMAN

PAT CRAHAN WAS skeptical when he arrived for his interview with U-Haul at the Skirvin Hotel in Oklahoma City. The day before, he had received a phone call from a U-Haul recruiter asking why he had missed his interview that day. Up until then he had not even heard of U-Haul. His only experience in trailer rental had been renting a Nationwide trailer (a chief competitor of U-Haul in the early years) when moving to Houston. Furthermore, he did not remember sending a résumé to U-Haul. "We [he and his wife] really didn't pay much attention to it," he admitted, a little embarrassed. "We really thought it was a solicitation, that they knew we were moving and that I had lost my job." The misunderstanding was resolved and, despite Pat's skepticism, he rescheduled the interview.

When Pat arrived at the interviewer's room, he watched the recruiter "wheeling and dealing in his T-shirt and khakis." It was quite a contrast to the elegant surroundings of a hotel known as the grand dame of downtown Oklahoma City, and Pat, fresh from an interview with the post office, wore a three-piece suit, an overcoat and a hat. If he had doubts, talking to the dynamic recruiter stirred his curiosity.

It was 1962, and the young Sooner had picked up work at a bowling alley in Kingfisher, Oklahoma until he could find more permanent work to support his wife and four children. By all standards, he was a prize hire for any employer. An Air Force veteran, he held a bachelor's degree in retailing from Oklahoma A&M (known today as Oklahoma State). His job hunt thus far had been unsuccessful. He needed a job, yes, but he would not sign on with just any company.

He and the recruiter spoke for a little bit. It was cordial, but probing. The interviewer truly took an interest in the prospective employee. Crahan took a few diagnostic and aptitude exams in fifteen minutes. The interviewer graded the exams quickly. When he was done the interviewer said, "Pat, you're no genius."

A bit surprised, Pat responded, "Mr. Shoen, if I were a genius, I wouldn't be applying for this job."

"I guess that's true," said "Mr. Shoen" and then he roared with laughter. Although Pat knew his name, he was unaware that the man interviewing him was the co-founder and president of U-Haul, L.S. "Sam" Shoen. Once he composed himself, Sam offered Pat the job of president of U-Haul Company of Oklahoma and Arkansas. The impressive title was lost on Pat. He was concerned with more pressing details, so he asked for references. Looking back over forty years later, he said, "I can't comprehend that I actually did that."

When he called Sam Shoen a few days later, Pat said resolutely, "You took a chance on me. I think I can take a chance on you."

Pat Crahan's interview was emblematic of Sam's personality. "I'm not very much concerned about the way I appear or dress," Sam said in 1954, "and if I didn't have to, I'd shave once a month." This is not to say he was a slob. The nature of the trailer business, at least in the early years, required constant road work from Sam, and this prevented him from being in business attire at all times. Sam also put little stock in the way a man was dressed, saying, "When I find a fellow who is primarily concerned with material things, I know that he is either immature or a fourflusher [sic]."

Sam Shoen was a "reluctant businessman." He had witnessed many failed business ventures of his father's. Of course, much of his childhood was spent during the Great Depression, when families huddled in soup lines, men rode the rails looking for work and business itself seemed like a dead end. During his childhood, his father gambled on too many make-or-break deals that broke. "By the time I was old enough to choose my own career," Sam said, "I had so many unrewarding experiences in the business world that I had definitely decided that the last thing I would attempt to do would be to make my livelihood as a businessman."

"I wouldn't say he didn't want to be a businessman," said Bert Layman, Sam's cousin and close friend growing up. "He didn't have a great deal of respect for them. He was very honest."

Reluctant to be a businessman, his experiences as a youth nonetheless prepared him for the eventual founding of U-Haul and the creation of the one-way trailer rental industry.

The arrival of Sam Shoen was as unique as the business he would create. His birthday fell in a leap year, February 29, 1916. He was the oldest boy and christened Leonard Samuel, the second child born to Samuel J. and Sophie Shoen, who lived near McGrath, Minnesota. Later, in grade school, a schoolyard game called for boys to refer to each other by their father's name, and Leonard became Sam, a moniker that would stick with him for the rest of his life.

His father was a former boxer and semiprofessional baseball player. According to Bert Layman, the elder Shoen was a gifted athlete who drew the attention of some professional scouts early in his career. With a new family, though, Samuel J. was forced to put aside his aspirations to play alongside Christy Mathewson and Ty Cobb.

AT THE TIME Sam was born, connecting the United States was difficult. The telephone was a convenience afforded mainly to those living in cities. Telegraph was still the dominant method of transcontinental communication. Continental travel was most effective via railroad. Although the airplane had been invented by the Wright Brothers in 1903, it was considered impractical and was used primarily in government service for delivering the mail. Roads were deplorable. The main highway to connect the nation was the Lincoln Highway. Built in 1913, and hailed as a milestone of American innovation, the Lincoln Highway did not live up to expectations. *The Evening Star*, a Washington, DC, newspaper, described the Lincoln Highway as "an imaginary line, like the equator."

On July 7, 1919, the U.S. Army, a year removed from its victory in World War I, set out to demonstrate to America a need for a better national roadway system. A sixty-two-day journey, by car, began in Washington, DC, and ended in San Francisco. One of the Army officers who participated in the trek was a major from Kansas and future president, Dwight D. Eisenhower. His report, like those of the other officers, emphasized that "efforts should be made to get our people interested in producing better roads." This trip stayed with Eisenhower until he became president, when he approved development of the interstate system of highways we now have today, a vital ingredient for the development of U-Haul.

IN 1923, SAM'S father moved the family from Minnesota to Oregon to pursue prospective business deals. The elder Shoen was described by his son as "'a Jack [*sic*] of all trades.' He is a man to whom the grass often looks greener on the other side of the fence. ... to this day he still intends to make a million dollars and retire."

One of Samuel's early ventures was in Shed, Oregon, where he operated a grocery store and gas station. There, Sam helped his father by pumping gas and doing anything else that had to be done in the store. In 1928, Samuel traded the store for a farm in Marion, Oregon. Samuel J. Shoen's venture into farming, Sam remembered, was unsuccessful ... no doubt because Samuel acquired the farm at the very early stages of the Great Depression, which would fully take hold by 1931.

The Depression hit the Shoens hard. "Sam had it worse than I did and I had it pretty bad," Layman said. "Sam always had a favorite story—how they hadn't had anything [to eat] for a while. There was a jackrabbit out in the field, and the whole family ran it down and clubbed it."

Hap Carty remembered the Depression years and the strain it put on families. "In those days, a lot of times when a man was out of work and looking for a job, he didn't take his family with him. He rode the rails," recalled Hap. "We had one train that used to go through the ranch everyday, and you'd see at least forty guys riding the rails. They were on the bum, but they weren't 'bums.' These were guys who were just out of work."

"I think his dad had raised his family during the Depression years, which is a whole different set of circumstances," said Hap of Sam's father. "He [Samuel] kept a family together and he did what he had to do to support them. That was a pretty good accomplishment in those days. He did it with instilled pride and all good qualities."

Farming itself was a precarious business. American farmers were feeling an intense economic squeeze. "Increased agricultural production did not stimulate an increase in demand. The result was overproduction, a disastrous decline in food prices. . . ." This was probably the problem that afflicted the Shoen farm, and yet another reason, in Sam's eyes, to avoid a life where goods and services were exchanged according to demand, be it agriculture or business.

The desperate conditions kept Sam away from school for days at a time in order to help his father or to work at neighboring farms. He did a variety of work, not the least of which was berry picking. It is unforgiving work that pays based on the quantity of crop harvested. It was during this time that he "learned a lot about winning while picking strawberries in the Willamette Valley." While other pickers might start out at a breakneck speed, he would pace himself throughout the day and "generally managed to come out on top."

Sam found diversions away from work, though. He participated in sports. Baseball was his main love. He did not have the professional aspirations his father once had, but Sam certainly inherited a competitive spirit from him. One example was demonstrated at a pie social when Sam was thirteen. He became involved in a bidding war in an auction for a basket lunch prepared by a girl he liked. She had another admirer, though, looking to keep her favor by purchasing her basket lunch. When the smoke cleared, Sam was the victor, with a final bid of eight dollars. Most baskets sold for seventy-five cents. Those eight dollars were probably Sam's life savings, but the bidding war was an example of his tenacity at an early age: to set a goal and accomplish it.

Shortly after high school, Sam, his father and sister entered barber and beauty school after inheriting a small estate from one of Samuel's uncles. Despite Sam's reticence toward entering the business world, his foray into barbering provided a glimpse of the skills he possessed, which demonstrated a keen business mind. He still disdained business, but barbering allowed him to finance his true aspiration of becoming a doctor, the next big goal he was determined to achieve.

In 1938, Bert Layman enrolled at Oregon State University, where Sam was beginning his sophomore year. Sam cut hair in his room for twenty-five cents to make ends meet. After making very little money in the first semester, the two of them met Julian McFadden, a local businessman, state senator and the father of Oregon horse racing. McFadden took the two young men under his wing. "I think he influenced us both a little bit," said Layman. "He was, I think, an extremely honest sort of person." They would sit intently through many lectures given by their new mentor. If Sam had an aversion toward business, McFadden, at least to some degree, alleviated this.

McFadden, aside from being a mentor, owned a hotel, and offered the basement of the hotel to Sam and Bert for a "nominal rent," as Sam recalled. "We were swamped," Layman said. Customers would line up fifteen to twenty people deep. The shop would open at 9 A.M. and stay open until 10:30 P.M. Sam, who was in class at Oregon State during the morning, would arrive at noon. The men worked nonstop, skipping lunch breaks in order to cut hair.

Their shop, while successful, caused controversy around town, and in some ways probably left a bad taste in Sam's mouth for unions. Corvallis, Oregon "was a union town," according to Layman. Sam and Bert's shop was nonunion. The enterprising upstarts offered haircuts for twenty-five cents, whereas union shops charged sixty-five cents.

When Sam and Bert applied for membership in the Fraternal Order of the Elks, other barbers, who were brothers in the social club, blackballed the two men. Sam and Bert were undeterred. "We made four times what other barbers made," recalled Layman, "but we worked four times as hard." Bert and Sam canvassed Oregon State's campus with business cards. They were constantly out marketing their services, which eventually drew substantial crowds of customers to their shop.

The business was so successful that it spawned a small chain of barber shops. This success provided Sam with a tidy bit of disposable income. He met his goal of paying for college and matriculating at the University of Oregon's School of Medicine. But the Japanese attack on Pearl Harbor on December 7, 1941 halted his growing business. "Before long," said Sam, "my barber shops [sic] were without barbers because they were all young fellows [who] either enlisted or were drafted into the armed services." He closed down his shops and resumed cutting hair in his room in order to feed himself.

Sam had been exempt from the draft because he was in the Navy's V-12 Program, which allowed young, draft-eligible men to finish their schooling on the condition that they became officers in the Navy upon graduation. The program ensured the Navy would have a fully staffed officer corps, and allowed universities to keep student enrollment up in the midst of a draft.

Although military needs closed one venture, they soon provided another: Sam and his father secured a contract for barber and beauty services at Camp Adair, an Army training post in Corvallis. "I was an inactive partner," Sam said. His commitment to medical school was time consuming. His father oversaw the day-to-day operations, while Sam did management work on the weekends. Lack of labor was not a problem this time. The Camp Adair shop employed thirty-five barbers and "four or five beauty operators." Another contract soon came Sam's way.

In 1943, on a trip to Hanford, Washington, where DuPont was refining material for the atomic bomb, Bert Layman saw "lots of people and no facilities to care for them at all." He secured a contract for a barbershop and beauty concession. He, Sam and Sherwin (Sam's brother) quickly formed a partnership for the Hanford shop. This proved to be very profitable, and, as Sam recalled, by this time he was "involved in two separate business operations that employed seventy men and several women."

Those who knew Sam at the time were unaware he was burning the candle at both ends. He kept up an illusion that belied the fact that he was working night and day to maintain his grades and social life and keep his business flourishing. "If I had a nickel for every time I stayed up all night studying medicine," he said, "I could throw a nice party." To his friends in medical school, he was known as "Slick" because of his ability to make a fast buck. If he was bothered by the negative implications of this nickname, it was not apparent. He enjoyed the fruits of his labor. Money flowed in and he was a big shot on campus. He owned a cabin cruiser on the Willamette River and a brand-new Mercury convertible.

In the fall of 1943, Mary Shivers, Ralph Shivers' wife, remembered seeing that Mercury roar onto the campus of Marylhurst College, a women's school just outside of Portland. All the girls in Mary's dorm would run to the window and peek out to see the ostentatious car and its flashy driver, who was there to pick up the student body president, Anna Mary Carty.

EVERY PERSON WHO knew Anna Mary and Sam said that the two balanced each other out perfectly. Such balance is apparent when contrasting their childhoods: Whereas Sam grew up facing constant economic tribulations, Anna Mary grew up on a prosperous ranch in Ridgefield, Washington, where she was born on May 20, 1922. Her pedigree was quite distinguished. The Carty family had been in Oregon since her grandfather arrived in 1840. Her mother, Mary Carty (née Fitzpatrick), before being married, had served as the first female postmistress for the state of Oregon, where she managed the office in Beaverton. William "Bill" Carty, Anna Mary's father, was a successful farmer and state representative. Both passed steadfast faith and ironclad ethics on to Anna Mary.

Her mother instilled in the Carty family a deep belief in Catholicism. This was no easy task in Ridgefield, Washington. For a while, the town held an unreasonable fear of Catholics. For its own protection, the first Catholic church was erected outside the town, and as Martin Carty (Anna Mary's youngest brother) recalled, when Ridgefield hired a teacher who was Catholic, the town was in an uproar. Mary Carty persevered. The family was heavily involved in their parish, and the values of this spiritual ethic remained with Anna Mary throughout her life, and would be the most indelible trait she would pass on to Sam.

Her father's political career flourished at a time when there were still politicians who, outside of the political machines of the city, were accessible: farmer-politicians whose campaigns consisted of attending socials thrown by various civic groups. Hap Carty, Anna Mary's brother, recalled with great pride that the most his father ever spent on a campaign was two hundred dollars. According to Martin, if Bill Carty received campaign contributions, he returned them.

Anna Mary's youth appeared blessed with considerable good fortune, but from the beginning she was dogged by a serious health issue. She had been born with a condition that affected a valve in her heart. Today, such a condition would be quickly diagnosed and treated. Such knowledge and technology did not exist in 1922 and so her condition went unnoticed until grade school, and then it was only a minor note that her heart beat half as quickly as the other children's, and occasionally she would suffer from shortness of breath.

If it did affect her in any way, she was not likely to say anything. Ducking responsibility on the Carty Ranch was unheard of, and William Carty made sure everyone contributed. "Being raised on that big ranch," said Martin Carty, "boys and girls had the same responsibilities. She was pretty active and strong. My dad did not discriminate boys versus girls."

Growing up, she was a model citizen. She skipped a grade in elementary school and proved herself to be a formidable debater. Her academic efforts garnered scholarship offers from various colleges; she chose to attend Marylhurst.

Although Anna Mary was a model citizen, she was not a bore. She enjoyed life. She had a vibrant personality that drew people toward her. She liked being social. Those who knew Sam and Anna Mary were not privy to what attracted her to Sam specifically, but given her outgoing nature and Sam's ambition and love of life, the two seemed ideally matched. Anna Mary was a woman on the move when she met Sam Shoen. Sam was on the fast track to success as well, and both decided to "hitch their wagon to a star."

Like her mother, Anna Mary was motivated, ambitious and smart. She majored in history and minored in home economics: a duality reflecting her passion for proactivity throughout society, and the hope of building a family. Her activities throughout her time at Marylhurst were quite varied, and indicated a person possessing a broad array of talents. She was beloved by the sisters of Marylhurst College, who admired her vigilant work in Sodality, a society dedicated to the devotion of the Blessed Virgin Mary. In her junior year, leadership called her into service when she assumed the office of treasurer for the student body. The following year, she was elected student body president, and with that honor came more duties. She became the vice president of the Western Association of Private Schools, and was a two-time delegate to the Oregon Federation of Collegiate Leaders. Although busy, she found time to appear in *Lady Precious Stream*, a Gilbert and Sullivan musical. In her final year at school she served as an attendant to Lady Marylhurst, an honor similar to the homecoming court at coeducational colleges.

Her tenure as president came during a "grave world situation," as the Marylhurst yearbook of 1943 pointed out. It was a delicate balance to maintain a vibrant campus in the throes of war. According to the yearbook, "These [assemblies] were important and in harmony with the international crisis, but the true cultural life of Marylhurst was not subordinated." The person responsible for it was Anna Mary, whom the yearbook was quick to praise: "The student body had in its president an able administrator, one who has a faculty for leading active, articulate meetings. Anna Mary Carty and the other student body officers deserve much credit for their capable handling of student government." Anna Mary distinguished herself as among the nation's best young women. She was listed in *Who's Who in American Universities.* She was organized, focused, inspirational and compassionate.

"Anna Mary," said Martin, "had she chosen not to have raised a family, there would've been no limits as to where she would've gone."

What compelled her mother, though, also compelled Anna Mary. Her mother, at the age of nineteen, had given up her position as postmistress of Beaverton to start a family. Anna Mary had the same compulsion. She had plenty of potential, but according to Martin, her life's goal "was to raise a family who loved each other, and was happy." Sam seemed to her to be the right partner for this endeavor.

The courtship between Sam and Anna Mary was, by no stretch of the imagination, romantic. He admits that when he met Anna Mary, he was "selfish, calculating, and immune to women." Nonetheless, something about her intrigued him. He set in motion a "six-month plan of attack" to put himself in position to marry her. When she needed an apartment, Sam arranged for her to live with his sister Pat. If another gentleman courted her, he steered the suitor to another prospective young woman. "I was plain calculating," he wrote. He knew she was the best thing to come his way. In October of 1943, he bought an engagement ring with a sole recipient in mind: Anna Mary Carty.

IN 1943, SAM Shoen experienced the most devastating blow to his ego: he was thrown out of the medical program at the University of Oregon for answering for a student who was not there. "I was utterly dejected," Sam wrote in a letter to his children, "and my pride was cut to the quick."

No longer in medical school, Sam was draft-eligible, and an enviable catch for Uncle Sam: He was college educated and had three years of medical education under his belt. The military would have someone whose medical knowledge was as deep as any medic serving at the time. This new set of circumstances caused Sam to reassess his life and propose to Anna Mary. One week later, on February 4, 1944, they were married.

"I insisted on an immediate marriage, which meant she did not have the wedding with trimmings all the girls really want," Sam wrote with a pang of regret. Sam was a conscript, deprived of his dream to be an MD, and thoroughly demoralized. When considering these circumstances, it is understandable when he wrote of his state of being at the time of the marriage, "I was a zombie..."

If the romanticism associated with marriage was lost on Sam, it seemed not to be lost on Anna Mary. Even today her smile comes alive in the photos from the wedding. It is obvious she did not have the trimmings of the traditional bride. The couple stands side by side, Anna Mary dressed in a jacket and skirt, not the traditional white dress with the flowing train. The only white is provided by a corsage pinned to her left shoulder; Sam is in his Navy uniform, a soft smile across his face. It looks like a photo for a prom rather than a wedding. But Anna Mary's smile stands out as an expression of hope in that somber time of war, as if she knew what was coming. She seemed to realize that Sam, although humbled, was by no means beaten.

According to Sam, the honeymoon comprised a few brief days together in Portland, before he went to boot camp at Farragut Naval Base near Sandpoint, Idaho. In *You and Me*, Sam does not try to embellish his record. He was stateside for the duration of his service. Much of that time, he was laid up in the hospital. He contracted scarlet fever while at Farragut, and in the winter of 1944, he contracted rheumatic fever in Seattle. Consequently, the Navy sent him to Corona, California to convalesce. He remained there until he was discharged in 1945. Anna Mary was always with him.

It would have been simple enough for Anna Mary to have stayed in Ridgefield on her parents' ranch, but she traveled with

Sam to wherever he was assigned. She made all the arrangements for these moves and visited him while he was sick. "She went to untold trouble to visit me during the several months I was hospitalized," Sam wrote, "and I would blow my stack if she was a few minutes late." Adding to her stress at this time was the impending arrival of their first child.

The fact that Anna Mary chose to have children posed a significant risk to her health. Sam was well aware of her heart condition. His medical training had taught him what to listen for when using a stethoscope. When he first listened to her heart, he "didn't believe she could survive one pregnancy." What he heard "sounded like a waterfall." When the two did talk about the future and children, Anna Mary was adamant in adhering to her Catholic belief that children should arrive as they will: no contraception. Those were the ground rules she set before marriage. "She had absolute faith in God," Sam wrote, but the doctor in him wanted a second opinion.

While they were still dating, in 1943, Sam and Anna Mary had consulted Dr. Hans Haney, a heart specialist at the University of Oregon School of Medicine. Anna Mary (Sam was assured) could have children. Sam put aside his fears and a day after their first anniversary, February 26, 1945, Samuel William was born without complications to either mother or child.

DURING HIS TIME in the Navy, Sam was still in a funk. Only a year before, he was a glitzy man-about-town, a year away from becoming an MD. Now he found himself deprived of his dream and laid up in bed at a naval hospital. However, one unusual spark of hope glowed in his mind: he recognized the business potential of trailer rentals.

When and how Sam latched on to this idea is hard to pinpoint. According to *You and Me* and U-Haul company documents, the idea came to him while he was visiting Anna Mary in Los Angeles. He saw rental lots, and the proprietors of these lots appeared to earn a livable income from these rentals. The trailers intrigued

Sam, "especially from the standpoint of one-way rentals." Other versions of the story have Sam's brother-in-law, Bernard Shaner, towing a rental trailer to deliver some things to Sam's residence in Corona, and it was this incident that fueled Sam's interest. Bert Layman set the point of inception outside of California, in Idaho, when Sam used trailers to transport equipment between his barbering concessions.

As for the idea of one-way rentals, it appears that was inspired by the hierarchy within the military as it pertained to officers and enlisted personnel. "I wasn't an officer and I didn't get moved by the government," Sam said. "Therefore I had to think about ways of moving and then I conceived how you might organize a nationwide system of do-it-yourself moving, particularly on a one-way basis."

These various accounts illustrate the evolution of an idea that had lodged in the brain of Sam Shoen and percolated, to fully materialize on the day he was discharged from the Navy. Bert Layman remembered that Sam was brimming with ideas for potential businesses, but Anna Mary keyed in on the idea of trailer rentals and worked with Sam to develop the idea.

On the day of his discharge, June 20, 1945, Sam and Anna Mary loaded their infant son and their meager possessions into a car and began their move north, back to Oregon. On that drive, the young couple devised the logistics for making one-way trailer rentals a reality.

In Portland, within two weeks of his discharge, on or about July 4th, their first trailer would occupy a small area at a service station. Shortly thereafter, the name "U-Haul" was conceived, on a road trip to Seattle, although Sam could not remember whether it was he or Anna Mary who had come up with the name. By mid-1945, U-Haul was more than an idea; it was a reality. However, the long march to success was only beginning.

2

DO-IT-YOURSELF

ON THE WESTERN side of the Willamette River, across the Burn-side Bridge heading toward downtown Portland, Oregon, there is a large, brightly lit sign announcing that John Deere was founded in Portland. It is an ostentatious display in the city's skyline. Twenty miles up I-5, though, in the shadow of Mount St. Helens, sits the small town of Ridgefield, Washington. The snow-capped volcanic peak looms on the horizon. Down the main road into town off the interstate is a nature preserve owned by the U.S. government—all of it, that is, except for a nominal bit of acreage boasting a small, nondescript barn. This small area of land is all that is left of the Carty Ranch. There is little to convince passersby that this sleepy town was once a hotspot of innovation. Only one marker points to this fact. At the town's outskirts is a humble orange sign that reads, "Welcome to Ridgefield, birthplace of U-Haul."

When Sam, Anna Mary and their son Sam Jr. drove into Ridgefield in 1946, the idea of such a sign would have seemed as daunting as scaling Mount Everest. The town was as far away from success as it was from Portland. U-Haul had not proven a smashing success; although popular, costs of maintaining the business drained the family coffers. Ridgefield offered family, a place to stay and reduced cost of living, so Sam and Anna Mary could regroup. Yet with its perilous proximity to Mount St. Helens, this family drive mirrored the state of affairs for the idea of U-Haul. Sam's dream for one-way trailer rentals was fading fast.

The difficulty for Sam and Anna Mary's success with the company was the fact that there were no models to follow. Trailers, at this time, were sold, which meant that once a trailer was built and sold, it was no longer the seller's concern. In trailer rentals, not only was the upkeep of the trailer the dealer's concern, so was the return and the recovery of the trailer, as well as the renters' safety and satisfaction. It would take only one terrible accident to sink the reputation of the fledgling company.

"People think the first U-Haul trailers were the ones Sam and I built when I was home from the Army," Hap Carty recalled. "I know he bought his first few trailers from a welding shop in Salem, Oregon called Martin Brothers Welding." The trailers usually cost between $100–$150, a fair chunk of change in 1945. Although the price was high, the quality of the trailers was not. Sam called them "junkers." They were made by local welders and service station owners who constructed trailers in their spare time to supplement their income. Most of the trailers were improvised fabrications that used car frames and a variety of axles and tires taken from different cars, a disastrous impediment for someone needing to repair the trailers they rented.

"It might take you twenty minutes to replace a bearing," said Hap, "But it might take you two weeks to find it." In short, trailers were like snowflakes: no two were alike. The lack of uniformity in these early trailers was Sam's greatest headache and expense. "While we were able to rent trailers, and they earned a fair income, the expenses necessary to keep them operating ate up earnings." New tires were constantly required and bearings needed to be replaced. (While today this is less of an expense since uniformity in product allows things to be bought wholesale, this was not the situation in 1945.) The variety of the trailers meant that new tires, bearings or axle repair had to be done differently each time. There was no uniform procedure that could be listed in a manual. Sam was learning repair through trial and error. Needless to say, it was time consuming.

Acquiring the materials for repair was no easy feat either. In 1945, World War II was ending, but the government still rationed vital materials needed for the war effort, including the two most essential repair materials for the trailers: metal and rubber. "Tires were our biggest headache," remembered Charles Dreisbach, one of the earliest U-Haul System members. "We were always replacing tires." The tire problem would persist until the 1950s, when U-Haul acquired more durable six-ply tires. But the costs associated with repair "aptly illustrated why people who had been manufacturing these trailers and selling them had not been interested in the trailer rental business."

Sam did what he could to stay afloat. When he returned to Portland after his discharge from the Navy, he had only $5,000. He barbered part time and invested the earnings in the company. The demands of his family, though, were not something he could ignore. As he said, "[A] man who is married and starts to support a family soon finds he is shoveling sand against the tide." He was shoveling sand against the tide with his fleet of junkers as well. After only a few months, Sam and Anna Mary had spent roughly $2,000 buying trailers, and had little to show for it other than a stack of repair bills. Money was slipping away quickly, and Sam was finding himself exactly where he did not want to be: "behind the eight ball."

Sam had a choice to make: "I was in so deep into the trailer rental deal economically that it was either make it or lose the whole thing." He had to refocus, adjust and learn from what the first rentals had taught him. That's what led to the drive to Ridgefield to live with Anna Mary's family.

It would be wrong to assume that Sam felt defeated. As a child, he was called "Stub" by his parents, which was short for stubborn. He credited his father for giving him "the willingness to try something new and different and the confidence that I can do about anything." Successful people do not become such by what they do when things are easy; they succeed by how well they handle adversity.

The move to the Carty Ranch alleviated some pressures of providing for a family, but it would also allow Sam the opportunity to develop the essential qualities that would make U-Haul successful: uniform design and construction, getting the best out of every employee and a simple do-it-yourself (DIY) work ethic. The Carty Ranch would be the birthplace of the U-Haul manufactured trailer. The processes that were established there survive even today in U-Haul manufacturing.

It was a smart business move to withdraw temporarily from Portland. "Part of the reason for being at the farm was economics," explained Martin Carty. "Then there were some accommodations— a space for the manufacture of trailers, and no overhead. So that made it good for Sam and Anna Mary to start right there."

Sam and Anna Mary's prolonged visit was nothing out of the ordinary. "Sundays were when people visited," Martin remembered. "We never knew who would show up or how long they'd stay. So it wasn't a big deal that Sam and Anna Mary were coming by and staying. And it didn't matter for how long." Anna Mary's youngest brother was just entering his teenage years when Sam and Anna Mary arrived. For Martin, it was a thrill. Little did he know he would play a part in laying the groundwork for the reborn trailer company.

U-HAUL IS A prototypical American company because it embraced the DIY work ethic that has been the standard for so many American innovators. Yet DIY does not truly capture the situation on the Carty Ranch. Sam and Anna Mary had a young child; they had just moved in with her parents on a ranch, which required everyone to pitch in; and the two had to reinvent their fledgling company, which at that point seemed likely to languish only as an idea. It was a true balance of family and business.

The Shoens did what they could to help out. Sam wrote in *You and Me,* "I tried to make myself of some use around the ranch, when I was building trailers, but I don't think I succeeded." It is a small bit of modesty. According to Martin Carty,

"Sam, very indiscreetly, had a way of being a major part of our family."

His help spanned his knowledge. He would give haircuts. "His medical school helped, if anyone got a cold or was sick," said Martin. Additionally, Sam honed his labor-relations skills with Martin and his sister Margaret with an early type of employee-benefits program. "Sam created a point system. We'd get points, but it was never for doing what we were expected to do. I'd get them for helping my sister once all my chores were done . . . just going above and beyond." Sam would give rewards, small by today's standards, but thrilling to his new brother-in-law and sister-in-law at the time. "He would see that you saw a movie once in awhile, which in that era, seeing a movie was a big thing. You've got to remember, this was before we had TV," remembered Martin. "And it may be that he'd pick something up and brought it home to you, a trinket that had some minimal value. You've got to remember, a Baby Ruth bar, at that time, probably sold for a penny."

If the ranch needed supplies, Sam used his military connections. "He had a knack for determining what needs were on the farm," said Martin. "He acquired, somehow through surplus, government surplus, an enormous amount of metal fence posts. He transformed our thinking about fence posts from cedar to metal. It was like a new technology had just shown up thanks to Sam Shoen."

Most noteworthy, according to Martin, was Sam's constructions of an implements shed: "Until Sam and Anna Mary started living with us, all our equipment was stored outside in the rainy Northwest, and so rust obviously was prevalent. And Sam in his spare time undertook the construction of a four-bay implement shed; did the entire laying of the foundation, dirt floor, and constructed that by himself. That was while he was doing U-Haul stuff." The effort and quality of the work impressed Bill Carty. "When you haven't had an implement shed," said Martin, "and you get a first-class one, that's just like getting a Cadillac after you've been driving a Model T."

Meanwhile, Sam set up shop in a garage on the ranch. Today, it is the only thing that remains of the Carty Ranch. The term "garage" is a bit too simplistic. Like anything on a farm, buildings served multiple purposes, and this garage was also a storage shed for canned foods. Sam's work space was not large, measuring roughly twenty feet by thirty feet. With all the equipment in the room, only two people could maneuver in the space. Nonetheless, Sam saw that an assembly plant for trailers did not need to be a massive structure with billowing smokestacks. The simplicity of a trailer's design would be one of the key factors in the company's success.

WHILE SAM WORKED to make his assembly more efficient, using the trailers as marketing tools became a top initiative for the next phase of the U-Haul Company. "I used to paint trailers for Sam," said Martin Carty. "He paid me fifty cents a trailer. From what I remember, they always had that danger orange."

Prior to the move to the Carty Ranch, the trailers were not used to their maximum potential. According to Sam, "[Trailers] were in the main junky looking. There had been very little attempt to make them look attractive." The colors of the new trailers were danger orange and black.

"We got [the paint] from W. P. Fuller Company in Portland, Oregon," stated Hap Carty, who, sixty years later, recalled the place of purchase without hesitation. "It was a matter of safety. That's what they painted the highway trucks up there. The state [Oregon] did. That was Sam's decision." One story has it that the motivation to find a bright color for the trailers came when one of the early junkers was hit by an automobile. At the time the trailers were black and did not stand out on the road.

There was certainly a safety element to this selection. The new colors stood out clearly, but they served as a strong marketing tool as well. As Sam recollected, "These orange and black trailers, sitting at different service stations throughout the city in plain view, formed billboards of their own." It was nice, simple and effective marketing—something other trailer rental companies did not pick up until 1950.

The billboard effect came from the stenciled signs on the trailers announcing "U-Haul," "rental trailer" and "$2.00 a day."

Continuing the trend of collaboration with family members, Sam employed the assistance of Anna Mary's uncle. "My Uncle Mick took a brush and put the first letters on the trailers," recalled Hap.

These trailers, though, still had some kinks that needed to be worked out.

Initially, Sam contracted the welding of the frames out to local welders. The frames would then be brought back to the Carty Ranch, where Sam would assemble the trailers. Early on, this system hit a snag. Since the frames were put together by different welders they did not always allow for easy assembly. Dimensions would be awry, and Sam would have to refit the lumber or the axles. The process was hardly efficient. Eventually, Sam found a welder he could count on to fashion uniform frames. Yet even in this partnership, something did not sit well with Sam. It had nothing to do with the character of his welder, but rather the essence of the do-it-yourself ethic.

Sam admired the welder, a man with one eye, who was so efficient at his work. Eventually, Sam offered the welder a fifty percent partnership in U-Haul. The welder politely declined and simply produced the frames for Sam. This story was a staple for Sam because it "illustrate[d] the necessity of the manager of a business operation being able to do every job in the organization." This trait would be standard in every person who helped build U-Haul in the coming years, and most certainly in Sam because "a man must know more than the people he intends to employ or very shortly the other man will have his job or have his business."

This principle was soon clear to Sam. In December, he made a trip to pick up ten new frames from his welder. During the drive, Sam could not put out of his mind an advertisement that he had seen in the paper about a welding machine. The roughly seventy-five-mile trip to the welder allowed him significant time to contemplate the benefits and pitfalls of doing his own welding. Sam's dad was along for the ride, and in *You and Me* Sam alludes to the fact that he and his father were both intrigued by the gamble of buying the welding machine.

When they arrived to pick up the frames, the welder did not have the frames ready. He had been tied up building a trailer for someone else. Without the frames, Sam promptly canceled the order. He and his father answered the advertisement, and bought the new welding machine for $100. Sam was a gambler, a man who did not hem and haw before making a decision.

This new purchase had a long way to go before it would prove to be a beneficial investment. Sam did not know how to weld. This wasn't a problem, though. "I have had sufficient experience," he wrote, "to recognize that there is nothing so complicated that the average man cannot comprehend and learn to do." Although Sam's will was there, the welding machine itself needed 220 volts of current. Bill Carty arranged for the power company to get Sam his power. In exchange, Sam agreed to install utility poles leading to the ranch. By day, he dug holes and erected the poles. At night, he practiced his welding at a local high school.

In a matter of weeks, Sam was ready to begin building his own trailers. The magnitude of what transpired that December 1945 was not lost on Martin Carty. Of key interest to him was a purchase Sam made: "He pulled up to the garage, opened his trunk and pulled out a power hacksaw. Oh, boy, I thought Buck Rogers had arrived. Before that we had to cut the wood and metal by hand and that took forever."

But one of Sam's inventions stood out to Martin that was less futuristic than the electric hacksaw bought at the store. "On the farm we had a cream separator," said Martin, "and they were geared so that it didn't take that much effort to turn the wheel once you got it going. And Sam transformed that cream separator into a forge for the heating and bending of angle and channel iron. To see that thing that once had been a cream separator told you that somebody with some ingenuity transformed that thing from what it was to what he made it. That goes further in saying that the only thing that Sam lacked in engineering was a degree."

U-Haul was now a self-sufficient operation but the last bit of the mix was about to be added.

Anna Mary's brother, Hap, who was serving in the Army at this time, received a two-week furlough. Even at eighteen, Hap was a giant. He was tall and powerfully built, with broad shoulders. He had a good-natured quality that caused people to gravitate toward him. His little brother Martin was in awe of him. "If you were to ever list the ideal qualities in an older brother," said Martin, "Hap would meet every one." Hap's entry into the company proved vital to the success and growth of U-Haul over the next two decades.

Today, with all the modern distractions available at home, it would seem a bit unexciting to spend free time away from the Army toiling in a garage building trailers. Hap did not mind. That's what people did. Martin Carty put it into perspective: "We didn't have things like TV or anything, If you were home, you helped where you were needed. So helping Sam build trailers was the natural thing to do."

The land itself lent its help. Much of the wood for the first trailers came from trees on the ranch that were blown down by storms.

"I helped him for about a week," Hap said. "I still have the first paycheck he ever gave me. I never cashed it. I figured, he's my brother-in-law . . . you know, help him out." Hap did some painting and mounted wheels, simple assembly tasks. When asked about his initial thoughts about his new brother-in-law's idea, he said, "I didn't know what to think about it." But the two worked together and turned out the first ten U-Haul manufactured trailers. Not bad for two men in a week's time.

A spirited competition helped the effort. "The two of them, I think, were challenging each other to see who could work the hardest," said Martin. "It was like Sam was getting somebody, as luck would have it, somebody with the same thrust as Sam had. So it was kind of a 'We can do' type of thing."

The process was expedited by the assembly-line aspect of Sam's design. "He didn't want to be building trailers," said Hap. "He just wanted trailers that were built right. So as standard, the trailers he built had the same taillight, same wheel, same tire. . . ." This standardization also sped up and simplified repair. According to Hap,

"Instead of looking for three weeks for parts, you could carry the parts you needed in your hand." This would be a benefit to the company later on. "Anybody could be trained to do whatever you needed to do," explained Hap.

Pretty soon, Sam was turning out trailers quickly, and at a minimal cost. The trailers were durable and repair was cheap. Hap recalled one final obstacle Sam overcame in order to distribute the new trailers—the hill leading off the Carty Ranch. "The first company car was a sixty-horsepower V8 Ford," said Hap, laughing, "and Sam couldn't get up the hill when he was pulling trailers."

Martin concurred: "Sam's car wasn't blessed with a whole lot of power." With a little help and pushing from people around the ranch, Sam made it out of Ridgefield and began placing U-Haul trailers throughout Portland.

SAM VISITED SERVICE stations around Portland to market his new trailers. The biggest difficulty in this endeavor was convincing service station owners to let him place his trailers on their lots. At this time, his old persona from medical school, "Slick," returned. Sam could talk a big game. He convinced the dealers (agents, as they were known at the time) that U-Haul was a company that not only was going to be around for a while, but would be expanding. "I told our Agents [sic] that we were from California," he wrote, "and were going into the trailer business in a big way and would soon be operating a thousand trailers." In reality, U-Haul had "fifty good and usable trailers." But the agents bought it. Sam hoped he could discourage others from getting into the business by giving the appearance that someone had already cornered the market in trailer rentals. His boast had "the opposite effect as it looked like there was big money in the trailer rental business."

Sam's optimism was grounded in some exceptionally positive developments within the first six months of moving to the Carty Ranch. His trailers were prevalent throughout the Portland, Oregon and Vancouver, Washington metropolitan areas. During this time, U-Haul had its first one-way rental: Portland to Seattle.

According to Hap, who was now home from the Army for good, the gentleman who made the first one-way rental "was a bushwhacker—a guy who makes false teeth, but isn't a dentist." For Hap, this was a big step: "*At the time,* I thought it was our first big success." Over the next few years, though, Hap saw each first big success topped by a new "first big success."

Throughout 1946 and 1947, U-Haul grew slowly but steadily. Sam and Anna Mary realized that their growing family and growing business, now thriving in Portland, demanded that they live in a home of their own in Portland. Their second child would soon arrive. They rented a service station on Nikolai Street. Their home was in back of the station. Hap also moved in to help with the company. Sam and Hap would build about three trailers a week. Ironically, the man who owned the station suggested that Sam consider building and selling trailers to supplement his income. "He was completely flabbergasted when he saw what we were really doing," wrote Sam.

Although the company grew, it was only because, as Charles Dreisbach remembered, "They were putting every dime they had back into the business." The Shoens lived in quite a threadbare manner. They used apple crates for chairs and acquired a bed from a family member. While the uniform construction of trailers minimized repair costs, the trailers still needed regular service, and in order to build new trailers Sam had to purchase material.

Around 1946, Sam and Anna Mary devised the Mail on Monday Program. Just as the construction of trailers was uniform, so was the method of reporting rentals from the growing number of dealers in the area, which stood at twenty-five by 1947. The Mail on Monday Program cut down on Sam's commutes between Portland and Seattle to check dealers' rental records and collect revenue from the rentals.

Dreisbach, who was the first person Sam hired to do accounting work in 1948, believed Anna Mary did most of the bookkeeping prior to his arrival. One can assume that she tallied the new Mail on Monday Reports. (It is also consistent with her experience at Marylhurst, where she served as treasurer for the student government.) All this was done while trying to raise a family and serving as the secretary for the U-Haul Board of Directors.

For nearly a year signs on the trailers read Portland, Seattle, and California, when in fact no trailers were ever *in* California. But by the end of 1946, U-Haul had finally branched out to California. The trailer was a one-way rental to Los Angeles. Since there was no dealer in Los Angeles, Sam arranged for the customer to deliver it to Bernard Shaner, Sam's brother-in-law. The rental cost twenty-five dollars. "When he started one-way deals," said Dreisbach, "it was pretty risky. We lost some." The result of the first one-way rental to California echoes Dreisbach's comments. According to Sam, the first one-way rental "was trailer number eighty-one and we have never seen it since."

Sam was undeterred; he sent another trailer to Los Angeles. Shortly thereafter, he made a trip to Los Angeles to open a one-way dealership at a service station owned by Al Olson. Once again, Sam had to employ some cunning gamesmanship to convince Olson that U-Haul was for real. Olson asked Sam what kind of financial support was behind U-Haul. Of the encounter, Sam wrote: "Not wishing to divulge the whole truth and yet needing to substantiate my story, I asked him if he thought $100,000 was sufficient backing. He said he did and I dropped the subject." Olson's service station proved to have a long and profitable history with U-Haul.

The company was growing, but what U-Haul offered the American people was so new that the people with whom Sam shared his idea could not fathom the industry he envisioned. Still, his dogged determination and infectious confidence turned many doubting service station owners into believers.

By 1947, U-Haul had what Hap Carty described as its first truly big success, besting the first one-way rental: "Sam bought a lot for $500 on 88th and Foster. That gave us a permanent home base and the facilities that we needed. We could paint, weld, fabricate, plus we had a little office there." The lot was previously a lumber yard. There were no facilities in which to build trailers. In eleven days, Hap and Sam built the new "manufacturing plant" for U-Haul trailers, a structure twenty-two feet wide and sixty feet long. It resembled the garage at the Carty Ranch from which Sam had worked. The design underscored the idea that Sam discovered on the ranch: the simple requirements of a do-it-yourself work ethic stripped the process to its basic needs without sacrificing quality.

U-Haul was on its way, and those who knew Sam and Anna Mary were energized by the new idea, including his cousin Kermit and Kermit's wife Helen. "We thought it was a very original idea and certainly one that would build upon itself," Helen recalled, "because at that time, there really wasn't anything like that, that we knew of anyhow, that would allow a person to put a few things [in a trailer] and haul it behind their car and take it to wherever they were going."

The Carty milkhouse building, home to the first U-Haul Company manufacturing plant, where L. S. Shoen built the first U-Haul trailers and clamp-on bumper hitches, both his own design. (Gary Robertson)

The cream separator-turned-forge that L. S. Shoen used to fashion the first clamp-on bumper hitches used in the U-Haul System.

An early model U-Haul open trailer, circa 1946, with toddler Shoen and a feline friend.

Two early utility trailers are loaded for transport to a dealer.

The U-Haul Company's second manufacturing plant, built in 1946 by L. S. Shoen and Hap Carty in eleven days, at 8806 S. E. Foster Road, Portland, Oregon.

The Carty Ranch, 1946. The milkhouse stands to the right of the main house.

A couple loading up their rented U-Haul trailer.

A U-Haul trailer, circa 1946, with stenciling.

The Oakland manufacturing shop.

An inside look at the Detroit manufacturing plant.

Navy ROTC Cadet L. S. Shoen, then a student at the University of Oregon Medical School, 1943.

Anna Mary Carty, 1942.

Anna Mary Carty (left of bride) at her sister Margaret's wedding. Also pictured are Shirley Shivers (Stewart, fourth from left) and Helen Carty (Lyons, third from left).

Anna Mary Carty at her sister Margaret's wedding. Also pictured is her father, William Carty.

L. S. and Anna Mary Shoen's wedding photo, February 4, 1944.

Hap Carty, in uniform, holds Sammy Shoen while Hap's mother looks on, 1946.

L. S. and Anna Mary Shoen with infant at the Carty Ranch, 1946.

Hap Carty and Anna Mary Shoen with infant at the Carty Ranch, 1946.

3

A.M. CARTY AND THE TRAILER MAN

BY 1947, U-HAUL was something of an underground phenomenon. The new, reliable trailers were proving popular with a country that was on the move. Part of this upswell in popularity derived from Sam's salesmanship and focus on the future. As he said, "I talked in terms of what we were going to do and not what had been done. . . . it did create interest, and the name of U-Haul Co. spread across the United States because people who were manufacturing or renting trailers would hear about it from their friends or relatives."

The pace of growth was slow. "It just didn't go all over the country at once," said Hap. "The first city outside of Portland was Seattle." There, still new to the industry, Hap witnessed firsthand the power of the bright orange trailers. Hap recounted the story of Bob Smallwood's decision to become a U-Haul dealer. Hap went to Seattle with Sam to close out a Texaco dealer. "He [the dealer] and Sam had a few words," remembered Hap, "so we weren't able to leave the trailers there until we found a new dealer. So we went down the street and there's a little radio shop, wasn't blacktopped or anything, just, you know, like gravel and so on. And Sam made a deal with the guy who ran the place if we could park the trailers there, give, I forget, five bucks, or something like that till we could find another dealer."

Hap and Sam left and found a new dealer elsewhere in town. When they returned to get the trailers in order to deliver them to the new dealer, Smallwood did not want to give up the trailers. "The guy didn't want to let them go," said Hap. "'Since they've been parked here we've had people stop by asking questions; they've wanted to rent them,'" Hap remembered Smallwood saying. "But it opened my eyes. I was just a kid, but it really opened my eyes." (Smallwood went on to become the biggest U-Haul dealer in the state of Washington. As U-Haul grew so did he. Eventually Smallwood would become a fleet owner and stockholder.)

These trailers, parked in Seattle, in front of a store only by chance, were easy to see and clear as to their rental terms and price. Hap's story demonstrates a few things: dealers were easy to convince once they witnessed the attraction the orange trailers had for customers and "it was additional income that made their business a viable venture." More important, though, Smallwood's experience showed that the public was hungry for Sam's trailers. They needed only to be made aware that it was an option they could afford and be assured the product they paid for was of the highest quality. The trailers, as billboards, did this.

The company continued to grow. After Seattle, said Hap, came "Spokane, and then Pasco, Washington, and we had a dealer in Vancouver named Al Pepping. Then, I think, Klamath Falls." San Francisco, Los Angeles and Oakland soon followed. "Then, for awhile, [Sam] joined what was called the California Trailer Exchange," remarked Hap. "That was other people in the business, and they would send trailers one way to our locations, and we would send trailers one way to their locations. I don't know why that arrangement ended. I know that of the trailers they had, some were designed okay, and some were not."

By 1947, U-Haul had rental agencies in three states, the primordial shape of one-way rental plans, a home office and a significant manufacturing plant. It had all the trappings of a respectable company. Yet, the concept of the company—one-way trailer rentals—was so new that it was hard for people to buy into it. This was due in part to disinterest on the part of the early trailer moguls of the '30s. Disinterest in one-way rentals was mistaken for impracticality. The case was simply this: local rentals and sales were profitable enough to earn a decent living. Therefore, men past the prime of their youth saw no immediate benefit to creating a system of nationwide, one-way rentals. As Hap Carty said, "They had their Cadillacs. We were young and didn't know any better. We never got fat."

Such complacency probably came from a nearsighted attitude toward customers. The nation was infected by a desire to move, what the Germans call wanderlust. And Americans wanted to move. As Sam said, "I think I hit the trailer-rental industry at an opportune moment and I think I was particularly equipped to take advantage of the situation." History would support Sam in this claim. Postwar America was ready to grow. Americans no longer wanted to live, grow old and die in the same place. Returning vets were eager to seek their fortune wherever they might find it. From the 1940s to the 1970s, "roughly twenty percent of Americans changed residence every year."

"Here came all these men and women back from World War II," explained Ron Frank. "They had been to those places [Europe and the Pacific]. They weren't going to stay in these small towns. They wanted the beach in San Diego. They wanted palm trees in Florida. They wanted the Gulf Coast. They wanted a better life. And it was going to happen. Like the song said, 'How ya gonna keep 'em down on the farm after they've seen Paris?' They're not going to stay on the farm."

For the first time since the Great Depression, Americans were right to be optimistic. America witnessed a "quarter century of sustained growth at the highest rate in recorded history." People in the U.S. were earning, per capita, twice that of people in Canada, Great Britain or Switzerland. Such prosperity allowed for a significant growth in automobile sales. In 1945, 69,500 new cars were sold. In 1946, sales of new cars totaled 2.1 million. In 1950, 40.3

million cars were registered to 39.9 million families. As historian David Halberstam put it, "[Americans] were young and hungry to buy because they owned virtually nothing. They were prosperous but not rich. Above all they were confident in themselves and their futures. Now they were striking out on their own, going after their share of the American dream."

The unprecedented movement of the populace across the country combined with increased car ownership provided U-Haul with a customer base desperate for what U-Haul had to offer: trailers. But these were not the only factors responsible for the rapid success of U-Haul. Many American servicemen stayed on the West Coast, where U-Haul did much of its early business, because they "had discovered the blessings of warm-weather living." Additionally, "Americans were streaming into the suburbs, some of whose populations increased at rates of 50 to 100 percent in these years."

Helen Shoen, the wife of Sam's cousin and U-Haul pioneer Kermit Shoen, recalled seeing how people moved prior to U-Haul. "Well, it seemed to me like a lot of them had kind of handmade trailers, or you would see cars go by that were stacked probably at least half as high as the car itself," she said. "They would fix something up, rails or something, and pile that thing sky high because, as I recall, there really wasn't much of anything at that time. I'm talking 1945, 1947, 1948. This is when Sam really built his first trailers."

Sam was right. He had entered the business at the right time. U-Haul had a customer base that needed to move. Most of the other people involved in trailer rentals did business only locally. Sam, however, saw the benefit of a nationwide rental programs. As was the case in most industrial breakthroughs of the 1950s, Americans sought out names they could count on. U-Haul was not nationally known, but Sam and Anna Mary saw the value in providing rental trailers, available to all families no matter where they moved. The trailers would be safe and reliable, rather than a crapshoot that might endanger people during their moves.

Yet national expansion was difficult. There was no Internet, plane travel was expensive and long-distance phone calls were not cheap.

The idea of one-way rentals, although practical in the sense that America needed it, was, in fact, impractical in practice. The nature of one-way rentals made pursuing the idea a flight of fancy until Sam came along. His most difficult task was convincing potential dealers that his idea could be a thriving industry. But as is seen in Bob Smallwood's case, the trailers proved to be promotional gems in their own right.

Building an industry, however, is no easy task. Sam's work took him up and down the West Coast. His average workday was sixteen hours long. Anna Mary's was equally long, when the responsibilities of caring for a family were compounded by an additional six to eight hours a day spent working on U-Haul matters. Part of the travel load was alleviated by the Mail on Monday Program. "This weekly report," said Sam, "relieved me of the task of chasing up and down the country every week to collect the income from these trailers." Although, Sam's workload was lightened, he reinvested his time and energy in expanding U-Haul. He actively visited dealers to maintain trailers and open new dealers.

Sam's road trips are now legendary. He commented in *You and Me*, "[W]hen I'm left to myself, I live on hamburgers and sleep in the car." The existence was quite Spartan, but for good reason. A system of assembly was well in place, as was a system of distribution and revenue collection. There was, however, no financing system that was consistent and reliable to provide a steady supply of money to finance the manufacture of new trailers. Every penny Sam earned went to paying for new trailers.

Martin Carty went on an early road trip to San Francisco with Sam. His recollections give a firsthand account of the U-Haul Company's first fieldman: "We took that old Plymouth of his. My mother made a bunch of loaves of bread. Probably five, six loaves of bread, a jar of peanut butter and a brick of cheese. And we didn't have sleeping bags, but every good farm had quilts and we took quilts with us, and we slept in fields. And then we washed up in service stations and like that cleaned up. He was on a shoestring. We slept in fields and ate out of a trunk."

The trip lasted a week, and was intended to open more dealers, but repair consumed much of their time. As Martin recalled, "There were always taillights [in need of repair] and of course at that time, he used safety pins to connect the taillight wires to the vehicle. It wasn't easy to get new dealers. Most of the stuff he was doing was just done on a handshake. He spent a lot of time talking to service station people, and trying to sell them on the idea that he had of renting trailers. He had to convince them that he was legitimate, and that he could supply them with trailers, and of course he could only supply them with trailers if he could rent them in Portland and go to San Francisco." If rejected, Sam never got down on himself. "He might try to get in the last word," said Martin, "but he was never dejected."

Sam tried to reward Martin's effort. "The last night down there," said Martin, "he was going to treat me to some fun, so we went to an amusement park. And we were dressed, I think Sam had khakis on and I had jeans or khakis on—anyways, the admissions place concluded that we weren't dressed good enough to go in. No amusement park. We went back to where we were sacked out in a field and called it a night."

Not all of Sam's trips are documented, but those who knew Sam and the early fieldmen agree this story is indicative of Sam's travels. It was the nature of his life. Sometimes Sam's late-night work attracted the police. He wrote: "More than one time I had to explain to the local police that I had a right to work on these trailers during the middle of the night. Some of them took a dim view of a character looking as rough as I working on a service station lot at two in the morning."

One-way rentals were an inexact science. Sam knew that the demand he saw was not confined to the West Coast. Nor was the migration of Americans one way into Oregon, California and Washington. By 1948, U-Haul advertised, "One-Way Anywhere." This posed a few problems. The first problem was computing a price. The second and most glaring problem was determining where the person renting the trailer would leave it once they arrived at their destination.

The solution to the latter problem is nearly inconceivable in this day and age: trust. Someone looking for a one-way rental was presented with a deal: The cost of the rental would be discounted by fifty percent if the customer promised to find a good service station, in a high-traffic area, at which they would give the owner a packet explaining U-Haul, and how the owner could now rent the trailer and keep a portion of the money from subsequent rentals, and send the rest to Portland. Today, such a plan seems impossible, but in 1948, it worked. This is not to say there were no flaws. Trailers were stolen and abandoned. "If they didn't turn it in," said Dreisbach, "it's pretty hard to run down a trailer when you're not even in the same state. So we lost some trailers." As a whole, though, the effort caught on. "We must have set up nearly forty or fifty agencies throughout the United States in this manner over a period of nearly two years before we actually made contact with these agents."

Another apparent obstacle to this plan was the likelihood that another person wouldn't take on another company's burden. But as Hap is quick to note, the trailers were hardly a burden. "[The dealers] had no investment on their part," he said, "just their time, and extra space in their service station. When we first got into business with service stations, we would tell the dealers, 'Take care of your gas customers first.' We didn't want to alienate any business they had."

Computing the cost was a bit more troublesome, especially when one-way rental costs had to be determined for trips originating outside of Portland. Eventually, Ralph Shivers Jr., Anna Mary's cousin just beginning his long career with U-Haul, helped Sam create maps comprised of concentric circles that would easily show dealers how much a one-way rental would cost. A map had to be made for each dealership. A series of concentric circles radiated from the dealer's town, like ripples in a pond. Each circle covered a certain radius of miles, which accounted for a zone. That circle corresponded to a determined cost. At the time, the national network of dealers was small enough to allow for this process.

* * *

AT THIS POINT, in the eyes of the dealer, Sam was the "trailer man" and Anna Mary was the imperious executive in Portland known only as the no-nonsense "A.M. Carty," whose name appeared on the checks. "My wife was the big wheel in Portland, Oregon," writes Sam. "She signed her name A.M. Carty, and everyone thought she was some big executive with lots of cash sitting in Portland telling 'Sam the trailer man' which agent to crack down on. A lot of agents and people I did business with on the road thought I was unusually loyal to my employer and some of them tried to hire me." Considering Sam's attire, the ruse was easy to pull off. He was the only fieldman repairing trailers. His wardrobe consisted of khaki pants, a T-shirt, and coveralls for painting. If it were discovered that he was the owner, U-Haul might seem like small potatoes.

The reality, though, was that as U-Haul continued to grow, it needed more people. The company had hired part-time laborers to assist with building trailers. But by 1948 the company needed a support staff in the office. Anyone who considered signing on with U-Haul needed to know, however, that it was not for the weak willed. Hap recalled one of the first new hire's introduction into the U-Haul family: "Anna Mary used to take care of the business end of the books and that kind of thing. Finally they decided that they were going to hire someone to work in the office. Sam hired this gal to come in. Anna Mary came down to train her and after Anna Mary trained her for about three hours, the gal left and never came back." This might have happened because, at that point, Sam, according to Dreisbach, had at least "a half-dozen checkbooks." The accounting was done with ledgers and pens, and required hypervigilance to avoid oversight and misappropriation.

As ominous as it appeared, U-Haul held considerable promise for the System members. Sam told Dreisbach, "If you stick with me, you'll make ten thousand dollars a year," which seemed like an inordinate amount of money at the time. That was the direction Sam was going, and by 1949 he was bringing others on board.

* * *

CHARLES DREISBACH WAS one of the U-Haul company's early hires. He worked out of the Shoen house, handling the bookkeeping while attending college. It was part-time work, and in 1950 he returned to Baker, Oregon after the death of his father. A year later, Sam called Dreisbach. "He said he was firing his office manager, and would I come back and take it over?" remembered Dreisbach. When Dreisbach returned in 1951 he was shocked by how far U-Haul had come. "No question about it," he said, "U-Haul was growing every day. We were getting more dealers out in the field."

Increasing the number of dealers was an obvious standard of growth, no doubt, but Dreisbach measured success another way. "He [Sam] was bringing in trainees," said Dreisbach. "That's what he would do: bring these fellas in, and train them and then send them out to do various and sundry things. So it was obvious there were more people employed by U-Haul all the time. We needed more people in the office. [U-Haul] was growing by leaps and bounds. Sam was training most of the time. He was a good trainer, a good teacher, taught people well. He knew that it [U-Haul] would go if he got enough people involved in it."

After their training, most of these new trainees moved on to the shop and dealership in Oakland, California. The Oakland shop was an old service station Sam had purchased on the advice of Anna Mary. It was called a "shuttle station," and it resembled the rental lots of today. It handled rentals and repair, and had a trailer manufacturing plant from which the demand for trailers in the Bay area could be met without having to wait for delivery of trailers built in Portland. These were all the facets of the burgeoning industry that the new hires were required to know inside and out.

In some ways, Oakland was a boot camp for the new U-Haul recruits. Some of the major names of U-Haul who started out there are Hap Carty, Dale Webber, Ralph Shivers and Dale Graves. At one time or another they all cut their teeth in Oakland, only to branch out later and extend the System to the rest of the country.

Oakland was a gamble, but as Sam wrote in *You and Me,* "I seldom do a voluntary act without first calculating the odds and being certain they are in my favor." The real gambler was Anna Mary. In minutes from a May 10 board meeting in 1948, "Anna Mary Shoen made a report on the Company's agents in California. She suggested the Company attempt to acquire a Headquarters Location in both Oakland and Los Angeles from which shuttle business may be handled and minor repairs made on the trailers." The motion carried unanimously with the proviso that it "be done when the opportunity avails." By July of that year, the shuttle station in Oakland was operating at 1341 East 12th Street.

Sam and Anna Mary had their eyes set on dealerships nationwide. It was clear, though, that Sam could not be "the trailer man" across the country. It meant Sam needed more operations like the Oakland shuttle station. Oakland was an opportunity for Sam to cull and develop new talent, and, when the time was right, call them up to move out across the nation to set up dealerships and oversee the spread of U-Haul.

Sam was not one to instantly put new hires into positions of authority and prominence. Most U-Haul pioneers say they started out at the bottom. Helen Shoen remembered that her husband, Kermit, started this way, even though he was Sam's cousin. "Sam made the statement," she said, "that he sure wished he could find somebody that would be willing enough to start at the bottom; that everybody wanted to start at the top."

Dale Webber echoed Helen Shoen. "[Sam] was interested in people looking for a future and someone who wasn't lazy. He believed in work," Webber said.

Webber was brought into the System by his brother-in-law, Bob Clarke. Clarke was, perhaps, the first U-Haul fieldman after Sam. He is someone Hap holds in high regard.

"I think in the first ten years of the business," said Hap, "[that] it is important to mention Bob Clarke and Ralph Shivers, because they were critical guys in actually going out in the field. Our headquarters were Portland, Oregon; they'd go out to Pennsylvania, New York, Boston, wherever . . . open dealers and do company business—whatever needed to be done. There weren't too many people like that [who] ever existed."

Webber was fresh out of college and an Air Force veteran. He went to Portland looking for work with the railroad, but found work in any field scarce. "During '49 and '50, work just wasn't available anyplace, no kind of job," remembered Webber. "I went to work for U-Haul in April of 1950 in their shop, and the wages then were a dollar an hour. If he [Sam] had said fifty cents an hour, I would have taken it." Webber quickly rose through the ranks. He was in the shop for roughly two months before being sent to Seattle with Bob Clarke to do repair work. There, Sam told Webber of his promotion to running the shop in Oakland. Webber recalled, "Sam said, 'I'm going down to Oakland. I'm taking some lumber and supplies down and I want you to run the shop.' So I got in the truck and went with it."

Running the shop in Oakland was hardly glamorous. The role of supervisor in U-Haul was molded from Sam's belief that any supervisor must know how to do the work of those under him. Case in point: Webber did not know how to weld when he arrived in Oakland. "I taught myself to weld," he said. "When the day's work was done, and everyone went home, I'd stay and weld together a trailer." Webber took a great deal of inspiration from Sam. Although he was the owner of the company, he knew how to build and repair trailers on top of crisscrossing the country to expand the network of dealers. Learning to weld helped Webber maximize efficiency. "Me and Hap—there were three of us there at the time," said Webber, "we turned out sixteen trailers in a week, which was more than our Portland shop was doing."

According to many of the early shop workers, the assembly line was less job-specific and more need-specific. Whatever needed to be done determined the efforts of the people in the shop. Everyone had to be able to build a trailer by themselves. The multifaceted workers at Oakland proved exceptionally beneficial.

Ralph Shivers, new to the company, was working the lot with Webber at the time. He remembered Saturday mornings coming to work to a full lot of roughly eighty trailers. "They'd all be out by like 9:30 in the morning," Shivers recalled. "Some of them would come back and be rented out a second time. It was absolute chaos, but by God, we rented trailers."

Webber concurred. "We probably did rent that many trailers," he remembered, "because every Saturday morning, Jesus, it was full and boy, every Saturday morning—two hours they were gone." This experience helped groom the future leaders of U-Haul. They were just young men in their early twenties, but they learned the business, including the most important part: hooking up a trailer to a customer's car. That was no easy task. Each bumper was different and a unique challenge until Tom Safford, a man who would become the greatest innovator in design engineering for U-Haul, developed the universal hitch. "There for a time, we had the damndest conglomeration of iron in the way of hitches you ever did see," said Ralph Shivers.

Making hookups even more difficult was the final piece to the process—connecting the lights. Webber remembered this method all too well. "The first light hookups were safety pins. In those days the cars had big enough wires where you could stick a safety pin in them. It was pretty cheap to hook up a car," he said.

Back in Portland, Ray Robbins had joined U-Haul. Robbins is a unique individual; he worked for U-Haul periodically from 1951 to well past 1965. He entered and returned to the company at various stages during the company's first twenty years, and his perspective is interesting in that his sabbaticals allowed him fresh insight to assess the progress of the company.

In 1951, Ray was a high school kid. One of his friends at school was Ramon Shoen, Sam's youngest brother. "Sam evidently felt he needed a cartoonist–advertising-man–floor-sweeper at the time, and I could do all of those," Robbins said. The prospect of being in charge of advertising did not intimidate Ray because, as he said, "I didn't know what an advertising guy was, but I knew it had something to do with art work, so I figured, 'Oh yeah, I can do that.'"

Unlike many of the early U-Haul employees who were not aware of the young company before they started working there, the trailers caught the attention of the aspiring artist. "They were just these orange boxes that went up and down the road with stenciled maps on the sides," Robbins said, evidence of Sam's marketing at work.

Robbins recalled that his interview with Sam was to the point. "[Sam] said, 'Do you draw cartoons?' and I said, 'Yes I do. Here are some of them.' He laughed. I think he was my first fan. I always took it as a compliment from Sam because he actually laughed out loud and nobody had ever done that to me before."

Robbins' job was to create cartoons to supplement Sam's bulletins to dealers regarding loading, display or customer service. He excelled at his job. "I would just say, 'We're having problems with blowouts,'" said Dreisbach. "'Let's get a one- or two-page cartoon that would indicate how to solve this problem.' And he would come up with these cartoons. Eventually it became this little folio of these cartoons that he made. It was easy for these dealers to go through. Rather than having to read a whole lot of text, they could see pictures of what they should do, what they shouldn't do."

"You would try to get the idea across," said Robbins, who rode with Dreisbach to work every day. "You would do it in as funny a way as possible so they [dealers] were not only instructed in a particular thing but they were entertained, too. Otherwise, we felt they wouldn't read it."

Robbins worked at the office on Foster Road. The office was relaxed and that appealed to him. "I did not feel I was in an office," said Robbins. "I just felt like I was part of a family." He was especially impressed by Anna Mary. Until that point he had never dealt with a woman so prominent in a business operation and involved in the world of an office. "When you talked to her, she made *you* feel intelligent, whether you were or not," Robbins said.

He remembered Anna Mary and Sam's interaction: "He [Sam] was sort of a crazy guy anyway, and that was one of his appeals to me, that he was such an adventurous mind. Sam was just full of ideas; they would just roll out of him like crazy. She could evaluate them probably better than he could because she would say, 'Oh, yeah, good idea,' or 'No, no, no, no, no, what are you thinking?' I think she sort of kept him in check so he wouldn't go crazy," Robbins said.

Another of Robbins' jobs extended beyond the office. On many occasions he had to deliver parts to dealers around Portland. A job in U-Haul that was specialized did not exempt that person from learning the company inside and out. It was based on effort and know-how, a valuable equation to the company's success that survives even today.

AT THE CLOSE of 1951, the one-way trailer rental business was growing across the nation. U-Haul scrambled to get organized. Sending trailers to random service stations across the country was ineffective. Dealers often did not differentiate between the various companies, which led to multiple companies' trailers being rented out of one station. Additionally, organizations like the California Trailer Exchange split rental fees in half. Repair costs were disproportionate among U-Haul and the other member companies in the exchange. U-Haul trailers required little cost to repair, but other companies' trailers cost U-Haul more money to repair than repairing its own trailers. For companies like Nationwide Trailer Rentals and National Trailer Rentals, this loose affiliation worked. U-Haul, however, could reduce repair costs by servicing and renting only its own trailers.

Sam and Anna Mary saw problems with this new nationwide network, the same problems that afflicted their early trailers: it lacked consistency in service and uniformity. Despite being firmly established in only three states, the area Sam covered was vast and growing. At the U-Haul board meeting of November 3, 1948, "L.S. Shoen suggested that the company purchase a heavier type of automobile since he traveled approximately 50,000 miles per year and the light Ford repair car was not suitable." These conditions indicated only a small problem U-Haul would have in its growing System within a growing industry.

At the start of 1949, U-Haul underwent a considerable overhaul. The company began to look beyond Washington, California and Oregon. At the board meeting of February 2, 1949, "The advantages of effecting arrangements enabling the company to rent trailers on a one-way basis to cities outside the boundaries of Oregon, Washington and California were discussed. The fact that competitive companies offered this service had been a source of irritation to our agents. It was agreed that we were overlooking a lucrative source if some arrangements were not made to include the service."

The option of incorporating in each state was difficult because "the Corporation had no workable method of securing sufficient capital to make this scattered operation profitable, or for that matter to even pay the initial costs of qualifying the Corporation in the various states." Despite the discouraging reality, there was hope for a nationwide network of dealers. The attorney for U-Haul at the time, listed as "Mr. Allen," suggested that "a private individual be leased certain trailers on a long term basis. Said individual to operate a Proprietorship [*sic*] and to open up stations in widely separated cities throughout the U.S.A." Sam offered to "reactivate the U-Haul Trailer Company which [had] been discontinued on the formation of U-Haul Co." Sam's goal was to "establish a nuclei of agencies throughout the U.S.A. to which trailers could be sent one-way and which they could be sent back." The plan was afforded a one-year contract, and would be reevaluated after that time.

Nearly a year later, in a special meeting of the board held on December 30, 1949, the board established the groundwork for nationwide marketing companies overseeing U-Haul certified dealers. The notes leave no doubt as to why the move was necessary: "[R]egarding the exchange of one-way trailers . . . the dispatching company [had to] remit 50% of the rental fee to the company owning the trailer." Keeping track of the trailers, profits and dealer audits were becoming a nightmare for bookkeeping and because "disinterested third parties controlled the choice of a trailer to be rented." Finally, the reorganization would provide "a considerable savings in office work [that] would result from the modification of the present practice of other Trailer Companies who could discriminate against one another and who did deal with twenty [20] to fifty [50] other companies."

The new rental agreement gave the renting company one hundred percent of the rental fee. U-Haul would assure proper repair and maintenance of the trailers. From then on, U-Haul trailers would be rented only by U-Haul dealers and serviced by U-Haul employees according to company standards.

It was an innovative concept but by no means was it perfect. Roughly thirteen months later, in January 1951, a plan to put into practice the concept of U-Haul companies, incorporated according to state, emerged. A stockholder-manager would be placed in charge of each company to "increase efficiency and to lessen waste." The new plan would ease tax burdens and decrease liability. From the beginning and even in the present, accidents caused people to say "it was the trailer." It caused the company's insurance premiums to skyrocket. "We have had cancellations of insurance policies already," the minutes read, "and it is easily conceivable that we could 'get caught' without insurance or without adequate insurance and be bankrupted." The new system would create "smaller business unit[s] capable of being operated handily, and efficiently."

Simply put, the headquarters in Portland had too much to deal with in Oregon, Washington and California. As Sam reported to the board, an example of "the evils of the present loosely-knit operation is the retrogression the company has undergone in the states of Oregon and Washington. Two years ago we were doing more business than all our competitors combined. At present, there are at least two and possibly four competitive companies who are doing more business in these states than our company."

This new program allowed for more immediate responses, and more local connection, but it also demanded serious oversight and accountability. To do so required meticulous record keeping at the local marketing company and back at the headquarters in Portland. To assure proper oversight, the idea for what would become ARCOA (Associated Rental Companies of America) was born. At a February 6, 1951 meeting, the board examined "the necessity of effecating [*sic*] a more accurate and detailed allocation of income and expense involved in the interchange of trailers." According to the board minutes, the system devised in 1949 had increased profits for U-Haul sevenfold. Yet, confusion slowed efficiency. Sam introduced "the subject of a separate and independently controlled auditing Company . . . to act as a central coordinating, and organizing auditing Company between this Corporation and U-Haul Trailer Rental Company." Essentially, ARCOA handled the logistics of tracking trailers, paying dealers, legal compliance—the paperwork end of the business. U-Haul would focus on building the dealer network, training the dealers and fieldmen and marketing the product as effectively as possible.

In the next month, the concept of ARCOA was approved partly out of need and with an eye toward the U-Haul Company's competitors. "It was agreed," read the minutes of the March 1951 board meeting, "that some such organization was becoming a necessity for survival and for equitable business dealings with other Trailer Rental Companies.

"The fact that at least one other Rental Company, i.e., the Croft brothers and their associates had recently completed the organization of a central coordinating body or association and that the Tysdale brothers apparently had some sort of business organization which permitted them to successfully do business with other men and other Trailer Rental Companies was discussed.

"The need for a separate coordinating and regulating body to act as an intermediary and clearinghouse in dealings with other Trailer Rental Companies was conceded."

U-Haul had centralized authority but decentralized control. And while their companies covered only three states, the organization for a nationwide System had been established. Dealers were being opened at an increasing rate, and a central office would coordinate the exhausting exchange of paperwork associated with a growing company. In theory the initiatives for expansion were in place. In reality, there was considerable legwork to be done.

* * *

FINANCING CONTINUED TO be the U-Haul Company's Achilles' heel. If the company was to expand, it needed a permanent cash flow. U-Haul had already tried a variety of options. At the May 10, 1948 meeting at which Anna Mary proposed the Oakland shuttle station, Sam also delivered a bleak report about company financing: "It was not expedient for the Company to sell stock because of the necessity of obtaining permission from the Corporation Commission and the expense involved in the actual sale. W.E. Carty suggested that a private party loan be sought."

This was a common option for U-Haul to augment revenue. From the very beginning, every possible person with money was approached about investing in the trailer company. The man stenciling the early U-Haul trailers, Mick Carty, was one such person. "One time," said Hap, "Sam tried to get him [Mick] to buy half of U-Haul for five thousand bucks, and he turned him down."

At one point early in the history of U-Haul, Sam looked to his brother Sherwin for financial assistance to build more trailers. Sherwin created an additive for car batteries. Sam was certain this would be a popular product, and could provide a sustained stream of revenue for manufacturing trailers. According to Hap, "Sam was interested in trading half of U-Haul for half of the Double Power Battery Additive business, and Anna Mary put her foot down. She really was a regulator as far as doing anything that was really rash . . . like trading half the company off."

Outside investment was slow to come, and profits were eroded by taxes and repairs. At a March 1951 board meeting, "[t]he inability of this Company to expand itself from the profits remaining after taxes was pointed out. The fact that contrary to expanding and increasing our trailer fleet we would need to curtail the purchase of new trailers in order to remain solvent because the Company's current liabilities exceeded the amount of money that it could hope to salvage after taxes for 1951."

Despite the stark financial reality, there was reason to be hopeful. Sam looked to move forward. At the same March meeting the board resolved to "encourage the establishment of other trailer rental companies in states outside Oregon, Washington and California, under the name of U-Haul Co. and friendly toward this Company and with which this Company could anticipate exchanging one-way trailer rentals as it had been doing with U-Haul Trailer Rental Co. so successfully for the past two years."

The popularity of the trailers was both a blessing and a curse. Across the nation the demand was high, but since the only manufacturing plants were in Portland and Oakland, the East Coast and Midwest markets were hard pressed to survive. So in 1952, Sam took a calculated risk. Without assured financing, and with only a hunch that the East would prove profitable, Sam sent Hap to Boston to establish a new manufacturing plant in order to supply the East Coast market.

Such a move was no small gamble. Between 1951 and 1952, the nationwide system of dealers was on unsteady ground. During the March 1951 board meeting, the system of individual companies organized by state looked promising. At the annual stockholders meeting held on January 17, 1952, it was resolved that "the Directors of this Corporation fully study and investigate all factors pertaining to a 'spin-off' of the U-Haul Co. [an Oregon Corporation] into three integral corporations bounded by states in which this referred Company is presently in operation." It was the official step to consolidating the nationwide system Sam had been trying to establish since 1951.

That same day, the board resolved "to consolidate the Company's operation." It would handle business on a state-by-state basis. The minutes from the meeting acknowledge "the Company [had fallen] behind in the competitive trailer rental industry on the West Coast." Separate corporations, it was believed, would allow U-Haul to corner the market in each state. With ARCOA as the clearinghouse, each corporation could concern itself with its own sphere of influence. The board resolved to consult a "competent attorney" to "advise the Company's officers as to the best method with which to accomplish [the] best results, and make possible a more competitive basis for this Company to operate and [develop a] more efficient method of operation so that this Company could do a better job of maintaining its operation on a competitive basis in the State of Oregon as well as to hold up its part of the U-Haul–ARCOA system, which obviously had not been done in the past two years for lack of a competent management in the various districts."

Upon consulting with an attorney, as directed, Sam heard some discouraging news. At the February 6, 1952 board of director's meeting, Sam and Anna Mary reported on the results of their meeting with Dave Patullo. Patullo was a Portland attorney who taught at Northwestern College of Law, where Sam was enrolled. Patullo advised Sam and Anna Mary that "the spin-off or split-up of the Company's operations would simply result in tax litigation of some sort with the Internal Revenue Bureau. . . . splitting up the present corporation into Corporations [sic] by states would involve difficulties with the Bureau of Internal Revenue and would result in only more difficulty in operating of the corporation rather than less."

The meeting concludes with an ominous resolution: the efforts of the company were divided among three states. As a result U-Haul was losing out to competitors in Oregon. The board of U-Haul then resolved "that the company call a meeting of the stockholders thereof and that this matter be discussed again, and that it be recommended that the Company withdraw from doing business in the States of California and Washington, and that the Company confine its efforts to the State of Oregon where it could hope to effect an efficient and competitive operation."

During this time in America, many companies opened up and created new fields of commerce. But for all the business plans, attempts to finance and marketing campaigns, the most important thing new entrepreneurs needed for success was ambition. Maurice McDonald, one of the brothers who founded McDonald's, knew what was required to go nationwide. He said, "We are going to be on the road all the time in motels, looking for locations, finding managers, I can just see one hell of a headache if we go into that kind of chain." Interestingly enough, when the McDonald brothers received the financial windfall from their hamburger stands they bought Cadillacs and they were content. Ray Kroc, however, wasn't content with a Cadillac, and as Hap said, neither were Sam and the other people working for U-Haul. Sam was aware of what stood before him to build the company into a nationwide organization. He, like Kroc, was ready for the headache Maurice McDonald loathed.

It seems implausible for Sam to look east in order to improve the efficiency of U-Haul. Nonetheless, he gambled.

"What happened," explained Hap, "there was one dealer at 460 Cambridge Street, in Allston, Massachusetts. His name was Dick Davis; he ran a Mobil station. And one of the reasons L.S. decided to start building trailers back there was: Every week, when Dick Davis sent in his report he would say, 'I can rent twenty more trailers,' or something like that." It was too much for Sam to ignore. And so Hap was off, with a wife and kids in tow, and five hundred dollars to open up the East Coast.

GROWING PAINS

(1952–1959)

4

GO EAST

THE SUCCESS OF the Oakland shop proved to Sam that producing trailers in Portland and then allowing one-way rentals to serve as the singular method of cross-country delivery was impractical. It was not only product delivery that was problematic. Sam and the other fieldmen traversed the country, touching base with the new dealerships that were opening daily. An all-out effort was needed. Anyone who could get into the field was sent on the road to deal with the growing network of dealers. On the day he returned from his honeymoon, Ralph Shivers was sent out to service trailers, a trip that had him on the road for months.

At the Foster Road office, Dreisbach's main duty as office manager in 1951 revolved around communication with dealers to help curb delinquency. "As the new dealers were opened up," said Dreisbach, "I would send out a whole sheaf of papers as to what they should do, what they shouldn't do. We had this all prepared, and we'd just shoot it out to them as soon as we got their name. But there were delinquents, no doubt about it. Some guys were just slow getting their reports in."

The cause of delinquency was not necessarily malicious. Hap was quick to note, "If you're running a service station and you got a hundred dollars worth of bills and only eighty bucks, you're going to pay your grocery bill and so on. And I respect that. But you know, we've got to pay our bills too."

Most delinquencies, however, were dealt with over the phone, according to Dreisbach. Money would arrive, but not always on time. On the other hand, phone calls were not as effective as area representatives, as discussed at the 1951 board meeting.

Directing a nationwide system solely from Portland was inefficient. For those who knew and studied Sam Shoen, efficiency was what he sought in every part of his life. He ate meals quickly because the meal break diverted his energy and attention from work. One-way rentals needed a system that would extend from coast to coast. That way, interaction with dealers could be timely and regular, and would allow for a solid business relationship to form between U-Haul and its dealers. Consistent upkeep of the trailers would allow them to last longer. It was time to set into motion a new phase of the U-Haul plan, but instead of branching out, Sam decided to envelop the nation. If U-Haul were to become an intercoastal enterprise, Sam felt that a move to the East Coast should be the next step of a pincer movement, not the finishing touch of a crawl east.

The man tapped to do the job was Hap Carty. The company's success required monumental undertakings, such as the venture into Boston. On only five dollars a day, Hap, his wife Toni and their two young children crossed the United States to Boston. They ate hot dogs and camped along the way rather than stay in hotels. He was to open a new manufacturing plant on the East Coast, and from there establish a network of dealers. Symbolically, it was stroke of genius. U-Haul was making it known that it was not a local or regional company. It intended to cover the nation. Practically, this was a huge risk, and would require complete focus, sacrifice, a little luck, dedicated workers and a good leader.

That good leader needed to be a dynamic person like Hap. His personality was infectious (he was nicknamed "Hap" because he was always a happy child). He was revered by other U-Haul System members for his outgoing and pleasant, yet direct, personality. "One person I will always remember because he always whistled and he always sounded really happy was Hap Carty," said Helen Shoen. This esteem, combined with a remarkable work ethic, allowed Hap to be a lightning rod for the early System members at Boston Trailer. Sam was well aware of Hap's leadership. Years later, while having breakfast with Martin Carty, Sam said, "I'll get a little too riled up sometimes, and I'll fire people, and your brother will go and hire them back. And he's got the best damn people working for him." Stories like this abound, and they demonstrate why Hap Carty was the ideal candidate to open up the East for U-Haul.

Before he could go to Boston, though, Hap did his time in Portland and Oakland. "I knew what I was going to be doing in Boston," said Hap. "So I was thirsty for learning. When I got into Boston, I really knew what to do." He credited his preparedness to Dale Webber: "Webber had really a good crew, and he put out a good product, and he did it in probably less time than anyone else, as far as being an efficient operation. I learned a lot of skills from him."

When he arrived in Boston, things looked daunting. Hap had to find a place to house the new plant. Hap had an ally in Dick Davis, who would help him establish U-Haul on the East Coast. "Dick Davis was really a nice man, and a damn good dealer," said Hap. "He used to let me do repair work right in the bay in his service station. We didn't have a building yet." This was no small gesture. Service station dealers like Davis relied on those repair bays to be in active use; repairs were their major source of revenue. Hap worked out of Davis' station, opened dealers and looked for a suitable location for the trailer plant.

Fortunately, a trailer manufacturing plant did not need to be a complex building, as Sam discovered when he was at the Carty Ranch. "It isn't a big complicated deal building a trailer," said Hap.

"It's just a garage really," said Ron Green, one of the early Boston Trailer workers.

Hap found a small building in Dedham, Massachusetts (just outside of Boston, near Foxboro) located a few miles from the building that Boston Trailer currently occupies. He and his family moved into the shop. Their living quarters eventually became the office for

Boston Trailer. They lived just like Sam and Anna Mary had when they returned to Portland after Sam's discharge from the Navy.

"We had an orange crate, a refrigerator and one bed—and a hot plate," Hap said of the furnishings at his apartment in Dedham. As the network of dealers grew, many of them handed down furniture to the Carty family. This, along with prudent savings and spending, allowed them to fashion a tiny home right in the shop of Boston Trailer, to the amazement of his employees.

"I don't know how [Hap] lived there," said Phil Schnee, who worked at Boston Trailer, "because some of these guys came in and moonlighted and they were working at all hours of the night building frames for the next day's production, and Hap and his wife and his kids were there listening to all that noise, you know, the welders, the banging and stuff. It would've been annoying."

If it was annoying, Hap never let on. He remembered the moonlighters with considerable fondness. He counted himself lucky for having them and was in awe of their work ethic. "The first two part-timers—one was a fella named Danny Keegan," said Hap. "He stayed for, like, twenty-five years. He worked full-time at the New Haven Railroad. And then Woody DeLillo, he stayed with the company thirty-one years until he died. And he used to work full time for the New Haven Railroad. He also would be a fry cook at a restaurant, part-time and all. Those people back there were so industrious. I had hardly any friends who didn't have two jobs."

Even after U-Haul moved in, the shop still needed work. "I rented a damn big sander, a commercial job and got two fifty-five gallon drums of crud off the floor," recalled Hap.

The plant was turning out trailers, though. A few months before, Hap had sent for his crew: Don Shivers, Ron Green and Cleo Miller. All of them had paid their dues in the Portland and Oakland shops. They were young and willing to go across the country to an uncertain venture, with no real guarantee they would not have to pay their own way back. The risk was nowhere near the front of their minds. This was in part due to Hap's efforts: "I knew that if you had two dealers you'd rent twice as many trailers as if you had one. If you had four dealers, and so on . . . so it wasn't long until I had fifty-five dealers. I *opened* dealers. I had no problem opening dealers. They were my friends. And we created the demand by expanding the number of outlets."

If there was any insecurity, or the proverbial moment of truth, the people at Boston Trailer never considered it. "Failure was nothing we ever thought of," said Ron Green, "We knew we were going to do it. And we knew we were going to get them going."

Ron Green grew up next door to Sam, Anna Mary and their family. He cut their grass and even chased away bullies who were giving their sons Sammy, Mike and Joe trouble. Sometimes Green and his friends provided welcome recreation, a break from U-Haul, for Sam and Anna Mary. "A bunch of us neighborhood kids had built a softball diamond we used to play ball," said Green, "A couple times, even Sam and Anna Mary came out and played with us. They were a lot of fun, too. She [Anna Mary] was very active in all things, and had no problem throwing or hitting the ball."

Occasionally, Ron showed up to play pool at the home. Sam played billiards for relaxation. Ron Green remembered Sam's approach to pool: "The first time, Sam wouldn't play because he said he was reading the book on how to play pool and he made sure he read it before he started playing. He had the table before he ever read the book." This pool table also became a place where Sam would hire some of his younger workers, such as Phil Schnee, the fourth member of Boston Trailer.

Schnee remembered what Sam told him at his hiring in the fall of 1952. "You probably won't be around very long," Sam had said. "You're a young man; you're just looking for an adventure." Undoubtedly, Schnee was envious of his friend Ron Green's cross-country trip.

Schnee was not in the initial group sent out to Boston, but he was well aware of U-Haul. He and Ron were friends throughout high school. Since Schnee was only seventeen in early 1952, he could not work for U-Haul, but he was counting the days. "[Ron Green] had gone to work for U-Haul part time, after school," said Schnee, "and I kept visiting the plant on Foster Road, and some of these guys would be working at six, seven, eight o'clock at night and everybody seemed to be happy and I thought, 'Boy this would be a neat place to go to work.'"

By the fall of 1952, Schnee was working in the plant on Foster Road. Ron was back in Portland by then. There had been a disagreement between him and Hap. "He was unhappy with something I was doing," recounted Green, "And I said, 'So does that mean I'm fired?' and Hap said, 'Yeah, you are.' So I left. Later on we talked about it and he said if I still wanted to go home, when I got back to Portland I'd have a job waiting for me if I wanted it. And I did and it was."

Although he was not aware of it, Hap's actions were a perfect example of Lewis Dunningham's quote, which Sam included in *You and Me,* "The greatest force for making people bigger and better than they are now, is the belief that they have infinite potential for growth. Even when they fail us, we are to continue to carry and express the mental image of what they may become. To have someone believe in you, even when you fail, is the most blessed and creative force in the universe." Second chances, and the opportunity for redemption, or the simple promise that anyone could rise to prominence in the company was the most endearing quality U-Haul offered System members willing to embrace it.

After a few months in Portland, Green was summoned to Sam's office. The rumor was that he and Schnee were going to be hitting the road. As Schnee tells it, he had no idea where they would go. "I had thought that we'd be going into places like Auburn, Washington, which I didn't think was very exciting," said Schnee. "Oakland, California would have been nice because it has a warmer climate. Being an eighteen-year-old kid, I didn't know where I'd go. Houston, Texas was mentioned. But when Ron came down from upstairs with a couple of checks in his hand for $125 apiece for expenses, he said, 'We're going to Boston, Massachusetts,' and I thought, Boston? That's three thousand miles. I've never been out of this town except to go to Vancouver, Washington, which is just across the river. The next morning, at three o'clock, we were on our way to Boston."

Schnee had the adventure Sam spoke of in the interview.

Schnee was unaware of the circumstances behind the scenes that brought him to Boston. "[Hap] had requested Ron Green come back, and Ron asked if I wanted to go, and I said sure," remembered Schnee.

"[Hap] didn't want him at first," said Green, "Until Sam said [Schnee] was a friend of mine. Hap said if he was a friend of mine, he'd take him. That made me feel good." Clearly, whatever transpired between Hap and Green left no bad blood, and Hap was thrilled to get Ron Green or anyone cut from the same cloth out to Boston.

They left for the East Coast in the winter of '53.

WORKING IN THE early manufacturing plants (like Boston Trailer) required men who could handle adverse working conditions—extreme heat and extreme cold. It was grueling work. Dale Webber preferred the marketing end of the business over manufacturing. "I think of not being stationary, not spending your time standing behind the stinger and the welding machine, not having to stand in there and breathe the paint," said Webber, explaining his aversion to plant work.

Phil Schnee was aware of just how demanding plant work was. Boston was a different beast than Portland. Schnee learned just how different as soon as he arrived at Boston Trailer. "When we got back to Boston, we had to stop and see if [Hap] was home," Schnee recalled. "And he wasn't. Sunday afternoon, Sunday evening, wintertime, it's cold—where's Hap today? And he's over in the shop, and he's building tops. He and Don Shivers were building [trailer] tops, and it was cold out. It was probably in the teens. These guys were out there working their butts off. On a Sunday afternoon, a Sunday evening."

"If you were out for just a paycheck, you didn't last very long," said Schnee. The plant was not climate friendly. It lacked air conditioning. The building was not weatherproofed well, so wind and cold air easily found their way in. Work often moved outside regardless of weather conditions. "We had no paint shop," said Ron Green, "so we had to roll [the trailers] outside and paint them outside. Sometimes that was cold. Sometimes, you'd have a little moisture in the air line that would freeze up and I'd have to stop painting for a while and take it in and thaw out the air line so I got enough air to spray paint again." The wait took a few hours, but there was plenty for him to do. "You never were standing around," he said.

Once they did have a paint shop in the back of the building, things did not necessarily improve. "Conditions weren't that great," recounted Schnee. "We didn't have ventilation [in the building]— we *had* masks, respirators I think. Paint thinner was pretty much the stuff you use in glue. So after painting in the shop for an hour or two, you kind of felt a little high. You felt like you were floating a bit, until you just discovered that you needed to open the doors and windows. Especially in the winter time you had to do that mainly because you were going to end up with some brain damage." He chuckled. "It was fun. The pay wasn't great so you had to have fun."

When asked what made it fun, Schnee didn't hesitate. "I think it was the challenge of what we were doing," he said. "You know, building the trailers. Seeing the end product. That was the thing. That's why I enjoyed painting so much. After I became a painter, I was able to see what I was doing, right there; immediate results."

This is what many U-Haul people in the first twenty years have in common: there were no clock-watchers. If there were, they did not last long. Even when Don Shivers explained his hours, it's clear that work was fun for him. "Technically we were supposed to work eight hours a day but most everyone worked more," he said. Generally they worked the extra hours to get a head start on the next day's work: getting frames set up to weld, prepping tires to be fitted to bearings, and rolling nearly completed trailers into position for painting. That way the day didn't need to be eased into; the men at Boston Trailer could hit the ground running. It was something they learned while working in Portland and Oakland, the same efficiency Webber had taught Hap.

* * *

WHAT MADE U-HAUL such an ingenious idea was the durability and simplicity of the trailer. According to Don Shivers, "It's not high tech, just hard work." A trailer, at that time, needed a body, some springs, a tongue, axle and wheels, and people to assemble it.

Ron Green best explained how the trailer as a product was an ingenious route to pursue in terms of manufacture. "The way it was designed, built, it would last almost forever," said Green. "I mean most of them have. We've always over-engineered things—we've always built things better or stronger than necessary but they last forever. They're a good product for people."

"The division of usage and the specialization of ownership is what the rental business really is," said Hap, remembering a management bulletin written by Sam. "And in our case, L.S., early on defined that we wanted to have things that were commonly used and infrequently used. That makes a good rental item: If it has a long life, if it has appreciation potential. One of the first ten trailers we built—U-Haul built—cost $125. If you rent that trailer for forty years, if you put on new tires when it needed it, or new bearings or new lights, and you could still be renting that trailer, and sell it for $250 forty years later. That's an example of long life and appreciable potential. And it's one of the reasons why the trailer rental thing was a good selection for U-Haul."

The simplicity of the design afforded the assembly line flexibility of duty. At any time, whenever it was needed, one person could do the job of another. This platoon effort helped to quickly relieve a spot in the line that might be backlogged. Nonetheless, they all had primary duties on the line. "Cleo was the welder," explained Ron Green. "Don was the parts man. He would take the material, angle iron equipment, he'd have to punch holes through it for the rivets for the tops. And then my job was painting."

Phil Schnee was quite impressed by Don Shivers, "I can remember bending fenders," said Schnee in obvious awe. "Don Shivers, was a guy, he was—phenomenal strength—this guy could bend a fender by running the steel rod—metal—into a machine and turning the handle with the other and coming out with a rounded fender. He never used two people. It was himself!"

Once the frame and parts were ready, assembly followed, as Green explained, "and then Don and I would get together and then sometimes Cleo would get together and actually assemble this stuff once the framework was done." Everyone took part in the assembly, according to Green, even Hap.

Assembly sounds simple enough, but only because the process was streamlined. In the first stage, the frame for the trailer was welded together. Workers laid the metal in the wooden frame, which was shipped directly from Oregon to assure uniformity in all trailers whether they were manufactured in Portland, Des Moines, Oakland or Boston. The wooden frame rotated. Assembly was done while the trailer was upside down. "Just before you rotated it over," explained Don Shivers, "You'd weld the springs and stuff on it and the axle and then you rolled it over and put on the wheels and then you could roll the trailer around. And then you would put the plywood sides and such in it. Then it would go to the paint shop and then out the door."

At this point trailers had canvas covers. "I'm sure it was military surplus. It [the canvas] was, you, know Army, G.I., colored canvas that you put up over the framework," said Ralph Shivers, Don Shivers' older brother. People in the shops often felt like sail makers, repairing the covering constantly. "We got into the model with the Neoprene tarp in the front," said Dale Webber, "which was probably, I think our biggest mistake: making those metal trailers with the Neoprene tarp in there because they didn't take in to account the weather conditions of the North or the rainy season, where it held the water and then it would freeze in there."

Shortly around the time Hap went to Boston, metal hardtops became the standard.

"We bought them to start with," said Don Shivers. "Then we went to making them, and we had to have some sheet metal working—such things as brakes—a brake is what you use to make an arc in aluminum. Once we started making them we had to have sheet metal machines."

One of the early people building the tops developed the process into an industry unto itself. "I believe it was the guy who has

GemTops," said Shivers. "That was before there was anything such as GemTops. It was just across the street [in Portland] and down a few doors." GemTops now manufactures steel caps and lids for light trucks.

It is important to distinguish between metal and Fiberglas because many U-Haul competitors chose Fiberglas instead. Customers found that the Fiberglas-covered trailers, when parked in the sun, caused the contents to smell like the material covering them—an unpleasant odor. Additionally, Fiberglas tops were difficult to repair. Generally, if they were damaged they had to be replaced completely, and the damaged Fiberglas was not useful for scrap.

Boston Trailer cranked out trailers. Dealers, though, could not get them fast enough. Ron Green said the fieldmen never needed to distribute them. As soon as the trailers hit the lot, the dealers were waiting to pick them up. In some cases, the dealers did not care if the trailers were painted or not. They just needed them to fill a local rental and could have the trailer back later in the day. According to Phil Schnee, the struggle among dealers to acquire trailers could be comical. "We'd have four, five, six trailers sitting out there and there'd be dealers coming in from Maine, and from faraway places to pick up the trailer to take back to their dealership," he said. "I don't know if there were any fistfights. It was them saying, 'That's my trailer.' Here flip a coin."

The men at Boston in the early years were typical of the people working at U-Haul. To them, their jobs were fun. Granted, they were extremely tough, although as Don Shivers said, "When you're sixteen, eighteen, nothing's physically demanding." The right people found the jobs that were perfect for them, and it enriched their U-Haul experience for decades to come. "I was lucky in Boston Trailer," said Hap. "Those people I mentioned, Cleo Miller, Ronnie Green, Don Shivers and Phil Schnee, those guys have got like 150 years in the company between them." To this day they are still a tight-knit group. The Boston Group meets in Portland every year and rehashes old times.

By the close of 1953, U-Haul had 237 dealers and 5,274 trailers in their fleet, nearly ten times the number of trailers the company had in 1949. The Boston Manufacturing plant was thriving and rental agencies were springing up across the country.

Boston's production could go only as far as the money that was available for assembly, but they still had trouble meeting the demand for more trailers. In a 1954 article, Hap wrote, "My only complaint I have is the shortage of trailers." At that point, Boston Trailer Manufacturing built more than one hundred trailers a month.

Hap relied on checks from Portland to purchase materials. Sometimes the checks did not always arrive on time. "Everything had to be shipped or mailed," explained Ron Green, "and around Christmastime everything would get backed up [in the mail system]. There were some times that Hap didn't have enough money to pay some of the bills so he had to borrow from Don Shivers' checks because he always had three or four checks backed up ... or more. He always kept his checks. He was very frugal. I think we needed some welding rods. We were out of them. So he borrowed some money from Don Shivers so he could pay for them and we could keep welding."

The story was a source of amusement for Green and Hap. Don was always repaid. Things were tight then, although Dreisbach was quick to assert that the company never had trouble meeting payroll. Still, with demand what it was, production could not slacken. Whatever needed to be done, was, even if it meant borrowing money from workers.

It is ironic, though, that Don Shivers was happy to lend Boston Trailer some money. Don's frugality is legendary among the Boston group. When they went out to eat, he usually ordered milk and bread. If someone had food left over, he would ask if he could eat it. "He was pretty cheap," said Phil Schnee, "But only toward himself. If we went out, he was the first guy to buy a round of drinks for everyone." Under the advisement of up-and-coming finance guru, Dick Wrublik, Shivers invested nearly all his paychecks into a new plan that would supposedly ease the financial burden of U-Haul: the Fleet Owner Program.

5

SLOW AND STEADY WINS THE RACE

FOR ALL OF its success in the early '50s, U-Haul could not receive a line of credit sufficient to supply it with the capital to build enough trailers to meet the growing demand. "The banks wouldn't lend them money," said Jerry Ayres. "They said if you tie these trailers to a post so they can't get away, we'll loan you money." The solution was the Fleet Owner Program. It would prove to be the key element for the success of U-Haul over its competitors. Granted, this success was due in part to superior products, but with no capital to expand the amount of product, U-Haul ran the risk of remaining a distant third to Nationwide Trailer Rental System and National Trailer Rental System, the company's chief competitors.

In *You and Me,* Sam sets the inception of the Fleet Owner Program at around 1949. It was appropriately based on the program used to finance other cargo carriers, albeit on a larger scale in terms of volume. It was "used to finance railroad cars around 1900 and known as the Philadelphia Plan."

According to Tom O'Donnell, the idea came from Ray Curry. "[H]e brought up this idea to Sam because he was trying to get financing from the banks and they wouldn't listen to him," explained O'Donnell. "And so they came up with this fleet owner program [*sic*] but it has a pretty rocky start, too."

Although the Fleet Owner Program was critical to U-Haul Company's growth, its start was as tricky as Sam trying to tow trailers off the Carty Ranch

"[I]t was pretty iffy," remembered Dreisbach. "People had to be sold on the idea. They didn't immediately jump on it."

"Because people were pretty skeptical about putting their money into such things," said O'Donnell, "because trailers went off to Timbuktu, and they probably wouldn't see or hear from them again."

The basic concept of the Fleet Owner Program is simple. "You could take some money and put it [into a fleet]," explained Don Shivers, "and they had a bank that would match what you invested. So if you put in a hundred dollars, the bank would put in a hundred dollars. Then the bank kept all the income until their share was paid back. It didn't make any difference if it was one dollar or ten thousand. All the money went to the bank until they were paid off, which was always less than two years, a year and a half . . . and when it got paid off you had twice as much money as you put in."

In *You and Me,* Sam talks about the first fleet owner's experience. This person had purchased fifty trailers. "The first half of the month that this fleet operated, the owner received a check for nearly four hundred dollars, and the first full month that it operated, the owner received a check very close to one thousand dollars as his share of the earnings." In the book, Sam uses this anecdote to show how word of mouth allowed U-Haul to catch on; direct solicitation was not necessary.

Yet others remember it being a bit harder of a sell. "He [Sam] got this wealthy attorney to come out, and he wanted him to buy a lot of trailers," said Dreisbach. "He did wind up buying some trailers—quite a large fleet of trailers, and did very well on it, but he was quite skeptical. He asked a lot of good questions, good hard questions. . . . as to how he's going to be repaid, and all the problems you would have with trailers, the tires blowing out, people stealing them, just the practical questions. And I really think he did very well in it."

The early investors were not enough. The banks were not in on the program yet, so the people who could invest needed to have substantial savings. Most of those people were still a little skeptical for the same reason the banks were skeptical. "They would sell these trailers to investors," explained Jerry Ayres, "and then you would sign a contract with them that they'd give them back to him [Sam and U-Haul] to rent for a percentage of the income. But that was awful slow because there aren't too many people who wanted to loan you money on something that they couldn't [physically] see as an asset." The program was sputtering. The man to resuscitate it was a young man in the System who was doing inventory audits for the Fleet Owner Program: Dick Wrublik.

Even during his interviews in 1988 and 2005, Wrublik did not want to be made out as anyone of great consequence. This is a trait shared by many U-Haul System members of this time. Humility was a quality common among workers across America. Halberstam points out that with GM, "Loyalty among employees was more important than individual brilliance. Team players were valued more highly than mavericks. It was the duty of the rare exceptional GM employee to accept the limits of his individual fame . . . the corporation came first and the corporation bestowed wealth but anonymity on its most valued employees."

And while Wrublik's humility was genuine, it was impossible not to see him for what he was: the person who took U-Haul to the next level. Although Dreisbach left to become a priest before Wrublik took over the program, he remembered Wrublik. "I would say Dick would've been a good salesman," said Dreisbach. "He saw the potential."

"[U-Haul] got off the ground, as I was told in 1952, when they hired this young guy out of school who was a mathematical wiz and number cruncher," said Jerry Ayres, who was hired in 1956. Even by then, Wrublik's contribution was invaluable and well known among System members.

Wrublik entered U-Haul indirectly. Sam hired him to straighten out Patty Shoen's [Sam's sister's] taxes. "When I first went in to interview, he told me to go home and put on a suit," Wrublik recalled. It was an odd demand given Sam's penchant for dressing down. "I was twenty-three and wearing old man suits, but it was good because when I started selling fleets I needed to look professional because I was dealing with people a lot older than I was," said Wrublik.

The task of fixing Patty Shoen's taxes was a bit more daunting than just straightening things out for a simple college student enrolled in a few accounting classes. Wrublik had to make a presentation to the Internal Revenue Service on her behalf. He was only a junior in college at the time. It was a test, though, as Wrublik saw it years later.

"[Sam] said, 'Well, try this, we'll see how you work out,'" said Wrublik. "In other words, his was a fail-safe situation, 'I'll give you something I can't figure out and I can't afford to pay a lot of money to it, and if this guy can figure it out for practically nothing, I'm ahead.' If he had hired an accountant for that it would have cost him ten times or twenty times what I did."

This is true to Sam's modus operandi, by which he extracted the very best from all his employees, and found hidden gems in people who were not necessarily the obvious pick to handle a given task. As many people from this time attest, this was Sam's greatest gift: placing the right people where he needed them. As Hap put it, "Sam looked for and found what he called the diamond in the rough: entry-level people who became company presidents and leaders throughout the whole system."

When Wrublik went to work for U-Haul, he was still in college, and the Fleet Owner Program was going into motion. He worked 80 hours a week (40 at the office and 40 at a service station owned by U-Haul) and attended classes. "I had an hour and a half of free time a week," he said. At college, he was enrolled in twenty hours of classes, twelve of which were in accounting. It was a natural fit then that in his new role at U-Haul he should help out with the audit that was underway. "I was there, and I just got involved," he said. It was a mammoth task, one in which Wrublik worked with System members to save the company money and time.

Before the Fleet Owner Program could get off the ground, it required that independent auditors assess the company's assets. "I had trouble with the accountants," said Wrublik. "They were just wasting the money. We didn't have it. I did my job there as if it were my own money." Financial accountability and effective use of resources were mind-sets which helped him succeed later on when he built up the Fleet Owner Program.

"They wanted to count every bolt," said Wrublik. Obviously, this was impractical, so a deal was struck whereby, "We'll weigh one bolt or ten bolts and then we'll weigh all that we got and multiply it out; that way we don't count every one of them. Cut cost like mad," remembered Wrublik. Additionally, the auditors, needing to count each trailer, wanted to freeze all traffic in order to accomplish this. Once again, a more practical idea presented itself. "I sent out a letter to all of the dealers: On this date write down the number on every trailer you got," said Wrublik. "I did this two or three weeks in a row." Eventually, he compiled an accurate inventory of the trailers in the System without having to halt rentals.

Once the audit was underway, a cost analysis for producing a trailer was required. Up until that point such a document did not exist. "It didn't make too much difference when they weren't trying to sell them to outside people," said Wrublik. "If you're getting ready to sell them to outside people you've got to know that you're at least covering your expenses." Like the problems with the audit, the task fell to Wrublik, "[Sam] wanted to find out what I could do," he said. "Meryl Payne, who was in charge of purchasing, helped me. He would give me the supplies, and we would work together with the people in the shop and finally put together a proper cost list."

At the time Wrublik came to U-Haul, Sam was in a difficult position with respect to the competition. "[Sam] was desperate for money cause he couldn't build fast enough," said Wrublik. (Competition at that time was primarily from Nationwide and National.) According to Wrublik, "These other companies were beating him to pieces. He was the third man on the totem pole." The system of measure that Wrublik was referring to was the number of trailers.

Once Sam launched one-way rentals, Nationwide and National had to catch up quickly. "They hooked up with other people in different states. They were organized well to expand. All they had to do to expand was go talk to some other people that were in the local business. You can see why it was a natural way to grow," recalled Wrublik. This loose confederation of rental companies versus U-Haul was the classic tortoise-and-hare situation. Yes, National and Nationwide expanded rapidly, but the expansion was a given, considering they were adding dealers with stock already on their lots. The rental companies quickly increased their inventory of trailers just by adding local dealers. "While we're adding a hundred, they're adding five hundred," said Wrublik. "[Sam] was in desperate shape. [The competition was] so far ahead of us it wasn't funny."

The rivalry among the three was fairly acrimonious. U-Haul people wanted to squash the competition. The color that had the U-Haul people seeing red was yellow: Nationwide's color. Yellow was a forbidden color in the office. "Back in those days," explained Pat Crahan, "I mean, this sounds weird, but nobody would wear yellow. No woman working would wear a yellow dress; no man had a yellow tie."

Ron Green told a story that illustrates the rivalry: "Hap was having a birthday party for one of his kids. And he got a box of crayons for all the kids, and a picture of a trailer for one of them to color. One of the kids colored his trailer yellow, and Hap about hit the roof. He went around and took the yellow crayons out of all the boxes." From then on, there were no pictures of trailers colored yellow.

Years later Pat Crahan accompanied Sam on a trip to buy a plane. "[Sam] said, 'Take me out to the airport. There's a plane out there that I've looked at on a sales sheet of some sort. He said, 'It looks like one I want to buy.' So we go out to the airfield. They show him the plane, 'No!' He gets in the car. He said, 'You know why I didn't buy that plane.' I said, 'No, sir, I don't have any idea.' 'Cause it's yellow.'"

Sam downplays the rivalry in *You and Me:* "I don't believe that a person should ever proceed with an attitude of hurting somebody else, running a competitor out of business or beating another in a business deal. On the other hand, a good businessman is competitive, he wants to win, but like an athlete, he wants to win fairly."

Ron Frank agreed. "Our crosshairs were on: 'How can we make ourselves more productive, more convenient to the renting public?'" he said. "We never had in our mind how to put them out of business. Wouldn't do it if we were told to. Of course, L.S. and Hap Carty never told us to. We simply went out and went to work."

WHAT ALLOWED FOR the meteoric growth of National and Nationwide was also their downfall. There was no plan or concerted effort to build more trailers. If the rivals needed more trailers, they added another dealer with a supply of trailers. Sam, for his part, worked constantly, and as Wrublik and many others attested, he put every dollar he made back into the company, but that was simply unsustainable. The Fleet Owner Program was a beacon of hope for increased revenue, and a massive push to build more trailers.

Once the program met all the necessary legal obligations, it was time to sell. "We hired this stockbroker, professional, middle-aged person, who was well experienced," said Wrublik. "He made one sale to a friend of Sam's. So he wasn't making any headway."

Wrublik went to work. He was one of the early investors because, as Dreisbach stated, "he saw the potential," so much so that Wrublik invested three times over. He used $500, which he had saved to buy into his first fleet. Then he borrowed $500 each from his mother and grandmother to buy into two other fleets. Additionally, he borrowed from the bank to buy into his fourth fleet. (At this point, the banks were not on board to match fleet-owner contributions so investors saw immediate returns.) It was a smart move. "I went out and talked to people in the shop and talked with all the people," said Wrublik, "getting other employees to go together in a fleet, all of us buying one." His sales pitch was given substantial credibility since he could show that he believed in the program enough not only to invest, but also to borrow in order to invest further.

When Wrublik took over the program, it was a natural transition, "Sam got mad at [the broker] and said, 'I can't afford you.' I can't remember if he asked me to do it. I know I was already doing it." As was the case during the audit, Wrublik did his job on top of his other duties, without extra pay, and Sam figured it was worth taking the chance. "What did he have to lose?" asked Wrublik.

The answer is not a lot. U-Haul was operating in the red, according to Jerry Ayres. "I was responsible for making sure that the suppliers were paid. That was very interesting at that time 'cause U-Haul never had any money and had all these bills coming due. So I'd go to the treasurer and ask him for money on this thing. And I'd have $250,000–$300,000 worth of bills, and he'd say, 'Well, I got $20,000 here you can have.' So I had to go out, figure out, allocate it out to who I *had* to pay and who I didn't have to pay. There were several big companies that let us carry this for quite awhile. One of Goodyear's dealerships up there carried us on tires. We were six, eight months in arrears on that payment. Plywood was the same thing. We had two suppliers on that—U.S. Plywood and Harper Plywood. They carried us for quite a while. Whenever they'd get behind in their bills they'd call up the comptroller and say, 'Well, heck can we have some money?' and I'd get whatever I could get from the treasurer on this thing."

Still, the morale of the employees was high. "Nobody was worried about it," Ayres recalled. "If management doesn't worry, why should you worry, because that was their responsibility."

The program that Wrublik set out to build was one that did not give priority to big-time, outside investors. Clearly, that had not been working. In order to build more trailers, the company needed a steady cash flow, not a one-time, lump-sum investment. It is responsible investing, as any investment officer will explain: reliable, steady progress, instead of high yield because high yield involves high risk. Instead, Wrublik looked to build the program from within. It made sense; the people with the most to lose but also the most to gain were the System members and dealers. The focus of selling the program looked toward creating joint ventures rather than only singular fleet owners.

His plan was smart but needed constant attention. "I wrote to all the field people and told them anytime they ran across anybody to turn the name into me," said Wrublik. "Anybody they thought could buy. Work on the dealers particularly. Try to get the dealers. Work with the dealers because you're with them all the time. Just tell them about this program. And I tried to work with the fieldmen and get them started investing. They wanted the job and they wanted to see the company grow, so they did it. Then I sent stuff out to the dealers. I sent a lot of them a prospectus. So we were hitting the dealers and I tried to work with the System members."

Getting System members to sign on was an easy sell, as Jerry Ayres attested. "I was probably one of the bigger salesmen in that after I found out what it could do," he said, "because I think, too, if you invested in U-Haul you were more concerned about making it succeed. People that have no ownership have no real reason to stay."

Wrublik enticed people to pass names along to him, "I made a contest," he said. "If you turn somebody in, if they buy within the next year, I'll give you so many points. Points were converted to prizes that were family oriented. They liked that. As a result, these fieldmen would get something for their families." As he later noted, "I made them all my salesmen."

FROM A BUSINESS standpoint, the concerted effort to include System members was smart business. But the Fleet Owner Program eventually fulfilled a spiritual facet of Sam and Anna Mary's business lives. Many people who knew Sam and Anna Mary are quick to note that Anna Mary brought faith into Sam's life. Until then, he had been primarily agnostic. Bert Layman, Sam's cousin, said, "Sam never went to church until he met Anna Mary." Once he married her, Sam became involved in the Knights of Columbus, a Catholic service organization, and according Ann Lorentz he also belonged to the Order of St. Francis.

All of these facts seem to lend support to the assertion by Wrublik that once the Fleet Owner Program gained momentum, it was influenced by the papal encyclical of Pope John XXIII, *Mater et Magistra*. This could not be the case, however, because the encyclical was published in 1961, nearly ten years after the Fleet Owner Program began. There were, however, other papal encyclicals published long before *Mater et Magistra* that Sam and Anna Mary probably were aware of, such as *Rerum Novarum* (1891) and *Quadragesimo Anno* (1931). These writings came about due to the changing nature of employee and employer and the rise of global communism, about which the Catholic Church held an ambivalent opinion. On one hand the Church abhorred the communists' atheism and their refusal to recognize private property. On the other hand, they respected the communists' compassion for workers, and recognized that this was the ideology's main appeal for laborers around the world. As such, these encyclicals addressed the changing face of commerce in order to make sure workers were not left behind.

In *Mater et Magistra,* Pope John XXIII recounts the points made in *Rerum Novarum* and *Quadragesimo Anno:* "[I]t is today advisable ... that work agreements be tempered in certain respects with partnership arrangements, so that 'workers and officials become participants in ownership, or management, or share in some manner of profits.'" As Wrublik pointed out, his sales approach was to find the people who had the most to gain. If the company did well, the money it received would be given back to the people who had helped pay for the fleets. Later, company bonuses would be awarded in terms of a company fleet, a profit sharing of sorts. System members were quite happy with the fleets serving as their bonus.

Other companies used this approach for successful labor relations. Eugene Ferkauf, who founded the successful department store E.J. Korvettes, "paid everyone—including himself—modest base salaries, but he rewarded exceptional performance generously with bonuses and later, after the company went public, with stock."

People who knew Anna Mary confirmed that she regularly read papal encyclicals and passed them along to Sam. So it is not unreasonable to consider that some of the points made in these encyclicals influenced Sam. They supplemented her already rigid adherence to business ethics. This is not to say Sam lacked business ethics, but Anna Mary's understanding and application of them is a trait Martin Carty still remembered vividly. "I asked her assistance one time in doing a report for school," remembered Martin, "and she gave me some very good insight as to business practices, business rules, business ethics; and she was very firm on business ethics, I recall that. With everything you do there was an ethical consideration to it."

She had a compassion for the worker, which clearly guided the evolution of the Fleet Owner Program into an employee-benefits program. In just about every case, it helped young, growing families too. "It bought braces for my children," said Ron Frank. "It paid for all kinds of bills that you have with a family."

As the program succeeded, some people were making more in fleets than they were at their jobs at U-Haul. "There was this one rental company manager who was making, for a manager, decent money, I guess," said John Zuransky, "and given all those trailer fleets—every year we'd [the employees] get one—and he kept investing his own money into it. Towards the end he didn't care about his paycheck. I mean that was peanuts compared to what he was making on the fleets."

Zuransky himself benefited from the fleets. "I took the monthly commissions. I didn't reinvest it. It helped pay for the house. I mean . . . that was a godsend," he recalled.

THE PROGRAM PROVED to be a success with workers, but it did have kinks that needed to be worked out in order to soothe investors' fears regarding the security of their investment.

Fleet owners had to ensure that their investment remained roadworthy. "There were certain expenses you paid," explained Wrublik. These expenses were for repairs and licensing. Furthermore, there was a threat that chance might destroy the investment altogether.

Those costs were minor compared to a larger loss. "When a trailer got lost, that would devastate you," said Wrublik. A trailer could cost $400. If a person bought a trailer, and that trailer was lost, the revenue from the rentals was lost—$400 down the drain. In most cases people didn't have the money to purchase a new trailer. Whether or not the chance of losing the trailer was high did not matter. The very nature of trailer rental meant that at any time a trailer could be lost, stolen or wrecked beyond repair. The solution was as common sense and practical as trailers themselves.

"We had a special insurance program that if a trailer got lost, it got replaced under a certain basis so that you didn't lose your investment," Wrublik explained. "Or if you got into a major accident, it would be replaced without a cost to you. We were able to reduce the risk factor to the owner by insuring the loss and major accident. Fleet owners got charged a certain percent under a formula for the insurance."

It was an ingenious solution. As part of the fees, the owners were indemnifying themselves. They did, however, need hitches for their trailers. Without revenue to build hitches the new trailers would be unusable. It would not be practical to build trailers and then not have an equal number of hitches by which they could be attached to customers' cars. The solution was the same for hitches as it was for insurance. "They expensed that off too," said Wrublik. "The idea was to take away the shock expenses by a percent. Funneling the money from the gross."

The program was essentially risk free for investors and they jumped on board. The revenue allowed U-Haul to really crank out the trailers. "I would order the trailers. I'd make up what we needed for the year. And I had those orders going in there for these fleets whether they were sold or not," said Wrublik. It sounds crazy, but rarely were the orders not filled. Wrublik would broker joint ventures with System members and dealers in which he always invested. This produced what Wrublik called the "psychological advantage" that helped turn the tide of competition in favor of U-Haul.

In sheer numbers, U-Haul overtook the competition. But the shared interest among System members pushed the company forward in all areas. Plant workers worked to fulfill the orders. In some case, these orders were in part theirs. Fieldmen worked hard to maintain the equipment as best they could. Dealers, impressed by the service of their fieldmen, kept up their displays to attract customers, who would in turn rent the trailers and be satisfied and return to rent again. They wanted a good product across the board because whether or not they were their trailers, these people treated the products as they would if they *were* theirs, which in a sense they were.

1954 WAS A landmark year for U-Haul. In 1953, the company had put nearly 700 new trailers into service. By 1954, they put more than 1,000 new trailers on the road. Bolstered by the growing number of trailers, Wrublik went to various banks around Portland hoping to receive a loan using the trailers as collateral. The first two he went to said no. The third, however, was receptive. For nearly six months, Wrublik and other U-Haul officials met with the bank officers to assuage their concerns. What convinced the bank, though, was what had convinced others to invest early on: Wrublik's own personal belief and commitment as demonstrated by his investments. "I was able to take my records," said Wrublik, "and show him what was done, so he had confidence." The result was a $2 million line of credit offered to U-Haul fleet owners.

"We were accelerating like mad," said Wrublik. Fleet owners refinanced every year and bought new trailers. Wrublik worked to educate System members about refinancing. He maximized their capital in order to invest in as many fleets as possible. Soon, a shortage of trailers was no longer a problem.

Each rental company benefited from this program. "The state operating companies had no [significant] debt," said Wrublik. "So they could expand their facilities. They had a few mortgage payments but not much. They didn't have any assets because the trailers were being bought by other people." Expenses for maintaining the trailers were covered by the fleet owners. Overhead was very low. "That allowed them to put money into good advertising,"

Wrublik continued. Now, the state rental companies spent the majority of their resources on marketing. This stood in sharp contrast to the competition.

"The competitors were out there building trailers," Wrublik explained. "Each owner in each one of these was part of the same company. Each building his own trailer, designing it and making it entirely different. So when they came into repair it, they didn't have any drawings or anything else. They can't find any of the parts. They have to make them by hand. Well, when you have to make the parts by hand it's horrible. When we came out and we produce a van trailer, it's got the same thing. It's interchangeable. We didn't have to carry a big inventory of parts, and they were available. You didn't have to make them."

SOMETHING ELSE AIDED U-Haul in overtaking the competition: the economic situation of the 1950s. Contrary to popular belief, the U.S. economy of the 1950s was not always booming. "A recession hit the country in 1958, temporarily souring the atmosphere." Wrublik points out that once economic downturns like the '58 recession hit, Nationwide and National were crippled, proof that sheer volume of equipment did not equate to resilience. When the Fleet Owner Program began, Nationwide and National were able to consolidate a substantial number of fleets, but that was as far as they went. "Our equipment was brand new," said Wrublik. "[The competition's] best equipment, almost ninety percent of it was old. So that doesn't take too long to start coming out ahead. You got new equipment, better equipment, and dealers that care about getting the rental more than most people. That allowed us to move very quickly. And once you move like that, it's hard to come back. How are you going to get their trailers matching ours? The cost of repair would break them."

Wrublik deflected any credit away from himself. His description of events was very matter-of-fact, with no hint of bragging.

Ultimately, the Fleet Owner Program saved U-Haul and was one of the key factors that helped the company outlast its competition.

True, the '50s began with Nationwide and National far ahead of U-Haul, but Sam and people like Dick Wrublik looked to build the company through steady planning and investment, and more importantly from within. The Fleet Owner Program cemented the pride that the System members and dealers felt. They knew they were delivering a good product. The harder they worked to ensure the availability of that product meant financial gain for them and a positive experience for the customer.

As for Wrublik's protégé of financial planning, Don Shivers, he benefited greatly from his investments in fleets. In fact, by the early '60s, the income from the trailers was enough for Don to retire. Not bad for a plant worker at Boston Trailer.

L. S. Shoen at this desk, 1953.

L. S. Shoen with Russ Maxwell.

U-Haul dealer Ed Hansen (Needham, Mass.) hooking up a trailer, 1950s.

U-Haul trailers, circa 1954.

HOW MUCH CAN YOU LOAD IN A TRAILER?

A demonstration of how much you could load into a U-Haul trailer.

U-HAUL ONE-WAY RENTAL RATE SCHEDULE

A one-way trailer-rental poster.

L. S. and Anna Mary Shoen on the couch at home, 1952.

Anna Mary Shoen with five-week-old Mary Anna Shoen, 1953.

L. S. and Suzanne Shoen at their wedding, 1958.

Suzanne and L.S. Shoen with (left to right) Mike, Mary Anna, Sam, Mark, and Joe Shoen, 1958.

L. S. Shoen stands with a trailer at a service station, 1955.

A boy and his toy U-Haul trailer, 1958.

A U-Haul trailer sales display.

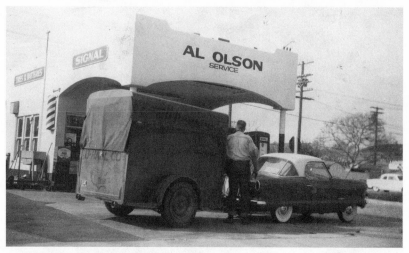

Al Olson, the first U-Haul dealer in Southern California, serving a customer at his service station on Pico Blvd. in Los Angeles, 1955.

U-Haul trailers waiting to be rented at an Amoco service station.

A U-Haul dealer and his crew at an early dealership.

U-Haul trailers for rent at a Sunoco station.

Ralph Shivers, Vince Fitzpatrick, L. S. Shoen, Ken Shoen, Bernard Shaner and Martin Zirbies at a 1952 training seminar conducted in Portland, Oregon at U-Haul Company headquarters on Foster Road.

Kerm Shoen, 1956

Vincent "Vin" Kiley, 1956.

The employees of ARCOA, Inc., the predecessor of U-Haul International, shown at company headquarters, 4707 S. E. Hawthorne Boulevard, Portland, Oregon, circa 1953.

Duane Swanson, 1956.

U-Haul fleet owner pamphlet.

6

GET IN THE VAN

IN THE EARLY days, there were men and occasionally a few women who embraced the romantic ideal of the road. For some reason, in the 1950s the road had an allure that captured America's imagination and spirit of unencumbered freedom. President Eisenhower, well aware of America's lack of a national roadway system, was impressed by the autobahn in Germany and knew America needed something similar. During his administration, America opened up in truly grand fashion with the interstate system of highways. In 1955, Eisenhower said in his State of the Union Address that the U.S. needed "a modern, efficient highway system" which he felt was "essential to meet the needs of our growing population, our expanding economy, and our national security."

On a smaller level, Jack Kerouac, a writer of the Beat Generation, captured the minds of young people across America in 1957 with his book, *On the Road*. Ted Morgan, a contemporary of Kerouac, wrote that the book "assert[ed] possession of a birthright . . . through mobility." A birthright many young Americans felt at this time, an urge to move. Within the U-Haul System, there was a small group of troubadours set free by a life on the road, who embraced a spirit of adventure—area field managers (AFMs).

AFM lore is rich and well documented, and the job is held in high esteem. The lineage is honorable, starting with the very first AFM, Sam Shoen. Later, as the pool of AFMs grew, each one never forgot the men who paved the way for them in the field. Today, former AFMs tick off the list of early AFMs as one would Hall of Fame baseball players: Sam, Bob Clarke, Dale Webber, Dale Graves, Ralph Shivers and Logan Frank. They quote Bob Clarke's *U-Haul Management Bulletin 25,* explaining how to live on three dollars a day in the field. AFMs were the go-betweens, dealing with ARCOA, U-Haul companies of the various states and the dealers.

Dale Green, Ron Green's younger brother and a painter who yearned to be a fieldman said, "I got to talking to fieldmen in and out of the shop, picking up trailers and various supplies, and thought that might be something I'd gravitate to. I liked the idea of being out and being on your own, working in a different area every day."

Similarly, John Zuransky, a longtime plant worker, occasionally yearned for the road. In the early years with U-Haul, he worked as a transport driver, moving trailers from one dealership to another. "I enjoyed that a lot," he said. "I got to see all of New England. I went all the way up to the end of Maine. When I first took the job, what did they do? They sent me to Albany. Oh, that was a big, big trip for me. I'm a local boy from home. I hadn't ventured too far from the city I grew up in."

Dale Webber's recollections of being a fieldman sound like they could have inspired the imagination of Dale Green. "It's being in the outdoors," said Webber, "doing the marketing, and being your own boss. That was the most important thing—being your own boss. Nobody told you when to get up and go to work. Nobody told you when to quit. So if a guy wanted to put in ten, fifteen hours a day he put in ten or fifteen. You just got paid so much anyways. And when you're on the road, what else could you do but work? And it was interesting. You met different people. You had to learn how to sell. You had to study cities. You had to know where to put those dealerships."

The AFM's job was made easier by the relationship he cultivated with the dealers. Often, as Dick Wrublik pointed out, AFMs brought dealers into the Fleet Owner Program. As the company started growing, the AFM became the first line of company relations between the dealers and U-Haul. So, while the job offered freedom, it did not mean a lack of responsibility. To be an AFM required self-motivation, discipline and the ability to handle being on the road under adverse conditions. The day might start at ten, because the previous day ended at one in the morning. Yet, the day that started at ten might end at three the next morning. Early AFMs were responsible for vast areas that encompassed multiple states, so a great deal of the workday involved driving.

One man, however, literally wrote the book on AFMs: Logan Frank. He is the man often seen in early editions of the *U-Haul News* wearing a bowtie and hosting dealer meetings in Florida. His contribution to the U-Haul speaking tour of 1962 brings a wonderful perspective on the life and role of the AFMs and their relationship to the dealer. There was no manual until Frank helped write it and codify it with his 1962 speech "How a Dealer Can and Will Do His Job." Until then, AFMs knew that they were to open dealers, service trailers and audit the rental records of the various dealers. Exactly how to do this was up to each person, but helpful suggestions would not hurt. Frank's role is also interesting in that he was the rental company manager of Florida for a while, before health issues forced a move to Arizona where he became an AFM again. This multiplicity of perspectives helped Frank learn how to make an AFM a person to be reckoned with.

"HE THREW MY application on the floor. I don't think it's down at the Towers now," said Logan Frank, recalling how Sam hired him in 1955. "He looked at me and asked, 'Are you an honest person?' I said, 'As a matter of fact I am,'" said Frank. "He asked, 'Are you afraid of hard work?' I said, 'No.' He said, 'How are you on punctuality?' I said, 'Not too good.' He said, 'Well, sit down and help me hire some people.'" They hired three more people that night.

Logan Frank was certainly a part of the generation Kerouac was speaking to—those who yearned to move. He was originally from Texas. After he married his wife, Dee, the two loaded up the car and moved to the Washington, DC area. A few years later, they took a trip to Miami, "It was like driving into paradise," Frank said, "so we decided we would then move to Miami. For the first six months we snorkeled and lived on the beach. Then we had to go to work." He saw an advertisement in the paper for U-Haul fieldmen. He showed up to the meeting, where over a hundred men crowded into a room to learn about their opportunities in the trailer business. "I finally wormed my way half-way down to the front. So he [Sam] picked out eight people to fill out applications." Frank was one of the eight chosen.

Anna Mary was with Sam. At this point she was a full-time mom, who worked on U-Haul from home. However, she made these trips with Sam to assist him in the hiring process. She was a quiet presence as Frank remembered but, "she was sizing us up," he said. Part of this process involved the interview stage, and the next evening a dinner with Sam and Anna Mary, to which Logan Frank brought his wife. This was not unusual, especially given the familial environment of the company.

The training process for Frank was a bit nontraditional. "The next morning L.S. met me and he said, 'Here's the truck. Here's a list of the dealers. I've got to leave town.' And that's it," remembered Frank. "He left town. So I had the list of dealers, and I knew nothing, absolutely nothing. But he asked me, he said, 'What it [the job] is, is going around servicing these trailers. Do you think you can do that?' And I said, 'Do you have others doing it?' And he said, 'Yeah.' And I said 'Then of course I can. If you have others doing it then of course I can do it.' I was a little bit cocky I guess at twenty-four."

The attitude was closer to confidence than cockiness. Frank had the background to pick up the fieldman's responsibilities pretty quickly. His past jobs gave him the skills needed to be an AFM. He had been a mechanic for Greyhound, which would help him repair trailers. After the Greyhound stint, he had been hired as a salesman for Wynn's Friction-Proofing, which taught him how to travel and stay active and involved in his sales accounts. Still, on his first call, he had no qualms about finagling a tutorial from the dealer. "I didn't tell him I had just started," said Frank. "I said [to the dealer], 'What was the name of the last fieldman who was here? What'd he do when he'd come around here? Did he really work?' 'Well, yeah,' he said, 'He worked. He fixed the ends of the wires. He aired the tires up and lined them up.' So I walked out the door and I said to myself, 'I now know what to do.'" With that, the the man who coined the phrase, "A fieldman to be reckoned with," set out to be just that.

IN "HOW A Dealer Can and Will Do His Job," Frank made a point (which Sam, in reading the document, underlined and highlighted with apparent exuberance) that is probably the most important maxim for a fieldman: "How well a dealer or the group does his job depends on how well the Fieldman [sic] does his job."

The job of the fieldman cannot be fully understood until the role of the service station owner, the U-Haul dealer, is better understood.

To those born after 1965, service stations have devolved into gas stations, places where people go to fill their tanks and maybe grab a snack. Originally, the service station offered *service*. People went there for oil changes, tire changes and other simple (and not-so-simple) maintenance. A service station owner was as close to his customers as a family doctor at the time. "When the automatic shut-off nozzle was invented," Hap Carty lamented, "that was basically the end of the kind of service station that made a damn good U-Haul dealership."

U-Haul itself was helpful in ensuring that service stations stayed open, through the commissions earned by the dealer. "[I]t was additional income," said Hap, "that made their business a viable venture. The average [service station] dealer that had U-Haul trailers didn't go broke nearly as often as the ones who didn't."

There was an appeal for the dealers to take on the U-Haul trailer besides the commissions, although the commissions were often enough to make car or house payments. The late Mike Morelli put the situation into perspective. Morelli was a Texaco dealer in Portland, and rented U-Haul equipment beginning in 1956. "When people move into the neighborhood with a U-Haul," he said, "if it's in my neighborhood, I'm the first person they talk to, and I realize that. First impressions a lot of times are your best impressions. If they had any problems whatsoever with the U-Haul trailer, or with their hookup dealer or anything, I always try to smooth it out right there. I don't call anybody. When they leave my station, they've got to be a happy U-Haul customer because they're going to be *my* customer. So, if they're a happy U-Haul customer, they're a happy, 'my customer.' I'm the first person they see in the neighborhood because they're in the neighborhood, and I'm the first person they're going to talk to. And I want to welcome them to the neighborhood."

This approach was confirmed many times over by other dealers in the System throughout the '50s. For example, Vern Snyder, a dealer in Northlake, Illinois said, in 1955, "I'm almost certain to sell gas with every trailer rental, either when the unit leaves the station or when it's returned."

According to Hap Carty, the job of the dealer often did not end once the trailer was hooked up and on its way. "If the customer ever had trouble with the trailer, you know, flat tire, or whatever, the dealer would go get him. Put him up in his house and feed him," said Hap.

Before a dealer was brought into the System, he had to be approached by the fieldman. And this was where the relationship began. Although dealers thrived if they rented U-Haul equipment, and word spread, it did not always equate to a warm reception for the AFM when they came to try and open a new dealership. Every AFM had to develop a sales strategy. These varied from person to person but they were generally clever and demonstrated the ability of the fieldman to think quickly on his feet.

"I'd go into a [prospective] dealer," said Ralph Shivers, "And he'd say to me, 'What are you trying to sell me?' And I'd say, 'I'm not trying to sell you anything. I want to give you something.'"

This pitch gave AFMs like Dale Webber a solid boost of confidence. "I was too young to be nervous," he said. "I just had the confidence that I could do it. In those days you sold the dealership on a chance to make money without investing any money, just investing their space and a little time."

AFM Ron Frank, Logan Frank's younger brother, had an approach that might have earned him an Oscar. "Occasionally, you'd find someone who didn't like U-Haul, for whatever reason," said Frank. "I'd introduce myself, 'Hi, I'm Ron Frank from U-Haul.'" To which a severe tongue-lashing, sometimes laced with profanity, would follow. Frank was prepared: "So I always had an address in my pocket for down the street. And I'd say, 'Did you think I was here to offer you a U-Haul dealership? Oh, no. Oh, no, no, no. You don't qualify. Do you know where this address is? I'm looking for this address.'" Then as he was pointing to the address of a neighboring service station, Ron would look around the service station, shake his head emphatically and say to them, "'You don't qualify at all. Please don't be confused. You don't qualify.' And several good dealers opened up that way."

Other AFMs took rejection personally. Jim Shaw, another great name in U-Haul lore, and a revered mentor for many young AFMs in California, spoke about his experience opening dealers, "If I went out soliciting dealers and worked hard at trying to get them, and I got turned down a number of times, that hurt," recalled Shaw. The multiple duties of the job offered him an escape though. "At those times," he said, "I could break away from that and go back to repairing trailers and get happy again."

Dale Webber dealt with it in a similar manner. He said, "If I was on the road for a week, which in Iowa, I was on the road for three weeks of the month, all the time, and I might spend Monday and Tuesday looking for dealers. And then Wednesday and Thursday repairing equipment. Monday if I hit a couple of dealerships and failed, I'd go repair trailers. But if I had a goal that that day I would open dealers, I'd open at least one or two dealers."

There were also polite considerations that AFMs had to be aware of. "I never tried to bother them on weekends," explained

Webber. "Because a service station is usually pretty busy on Friday and Saturday." This type of consideration would pay big dividends for an AFM and his dealers.

Working with the dealer brought many benefits. If an AFM did his job well, it brought the dealer rentals, which, as Mike Morelli asserted, helped the service station. This, in turn, compelled the dealer to assist his AFM. This was the case for Ron Frank, who developed a strong relationship with Al Maynard, a Texaco dealer in his area. "I had a map of Miami-metro, and Logan had put X's all over the map telling me where to open up U-Haul dealers," said Frank. "And so I went to Al Maynard and I said, 'Al, I got to open up a bunch of dealers.' And he said, 'Well, okay, where at?' And so I showed him, and he said, 'I know this man; open him up. Don't open up this guy.'" Ron was a little surprised by Maynard's willingness to see other dealers open up near his station. "I said 'Why are you helping me?' He said, 'Oh, you're just going to bring the equipment in closer and I'm just going to get it and rent it.'"

If an AFM handled his area well, dealers were often very rational about other dealerships opening nearby, sometimes across the street. Dealer cooperation was important to the growth of U-Haul. If, for instance, a dealer was out of trailers, he could send the customer to a neighboring dealer. "Our objective is to serve the public," Logan said in 1962. And having multiple dealerships in a given city was important to fulfilling this objective. Most dealers could fit only a given number of trailers on their lots, so others needed to be opened to fill the growing number of trailers being turned out by the plants. Dealer cooperation worked because of reciprocity. If one dealer lost a customer to another, he could usually count on that dealer who took that customer to send one his way later on.

Dealers took pride in the U-Haul product, and did what they could to put it in the public eye. Issues of *U-Haul News* from the '50s show pictures of dealers using U-Haul trailers as floats in parades. The November 1960 *U-Haul News* featured a photo of a string of U-Haul trailers in a Labor Day Parade in Coeburn, Virginia. An April 1959 issue showed photos from the Harvest Festival in Henderson, North Carolina. The caption under the photo read, "Gaily decorated U-Haul Trailers [*sic*] made up into a spectacular tandem float by the American Red Cross was a real crowd-pleaser. The trailers are donated for each year's parade by Hendersonville's U-Haul dealer J.S. Porter [32–14]." Examples like these are evidence that dealers were deeply involved in their community. U-Haul trailers were every bit a part of a municipality's social fabric as the dealers were.

The responsibility for making a dealership profitable fell squarely on the AFM, according to Logan Frank's lecture: "A field territory is only as good as the Fieldman [*sic*] running it." He suggested a few options for doing this. One was dealer meetings. Logan was famous for these after he became the rental company manager of Florida. These meetings generally occurred after hours and featured some snacks and drinks, and served as short training sessions for dealers. These meetings sometimes featured recordings of phone calls to dealers, done by mystery callers [often Dee Frank], to make sure the dealers were giving the appropriate sales pitch for the company. The meetings were vital for U-Haul. "The dealer was the best feedback we had as to what to do," said Hap.

The job was in some respects supervisory, but it was important not to be bossy. As Ron Frank said, while recalling a bulletin from Sam, "Service station dealers are bossed by the oil company, by the utility company, the zoning inspector comes by and rags on him. . . . He's got this endless list of bosses constantly carping and chirping at him. The question is: Is he also bossed by U-Haul? No, you don't boss the person, you build up their dignity. You build up their self-respect." Ron Frank's words also fall into Logan's advice from 1962: "No one ever really makes progress if he is told only about his bad points. People thrive on the properly placed pat on the back."

The mystery caller might perhaps have seemed bossy. In reality it was done for the dealers' benefit, to put money in their pockets. A 1959 issue of *U-Haul News* ran a two-page article titled, "Telephone Salesmanship Means Greater Rental Earnings for Dealers." The article points out, "If you lose one local rental a day, you lose $30–$40 of income a month. Lose a one-way rental each

day and you've lost several hundred dollars over a similar period."
Assuring a dealer of better revenue through a well placed pitch was
probably a welcome "properly placed pat on the back" as Logan
would say.

The relationship between the dealer and AFM was not always
harmonious. Some dealers had to be closed by an AFM. It was the
nature of the business. Generally, this was done because dealers were
not sending their weekly reports on time. Or in some cases they
were cheating the System. If problems did arise and a dealer needed
to be confronted or closed, it was presented not as if the dealer
worked for U-Haul. Instead, "you made it a personal thing," said
Ron Frank. "It's not that you failed to report to U-Haul. You failed
to report and you made your area field manager look bad." Even in
times of contention or dispute, a personal relationship was absolutely
necessary between the AFM and a dealer. Although it was professional, it was a tight bond, a symbiosis between the two parties.

AFMS WORKED FOR the rental company manager, later called,
marketing company president. These companies were organized by
state. Some of the smaller states were combined into one company.
The heads of these companies were not corporate yes-men. They
were, more often than not, local men who could relate well to the
dealers. One of the top rental company managers was Jim Shaw.
"Jim Shaw was another guy who was, in a sense, a *giant,*" said Hap.
"He had a thousand dealers in one rental company. He was very
knowledgeable. He brought a lot of good people on. I can't say
enough good about him. It takes *a hell of a good man* just in energy
alone to run a company that big."

One of Shaw's young AFMs was Dale Green. He still valued the
patience Shaw afforded his AFMs. "He gave you a lot of freedom
to do your job. Didn't pressure you that much," Green recalled. "As
long as you did your job right, he was right there with you. I don't
ever remember him getting mad at me. I think he was always trying to help you . . . positive stuff." This type of mentor relationship
often was the basis for success in the early rental companies.

Another policy that proved successful was former AFMs assuming the role of rental company manager, which enabled a smooth transition for the dealers. Case in point: Logan Frank and Jim Oakley. Logan ran Florida, while Oakley ran Texas. Their contemporaries emphasized that the two men motivated people differently. Oakley epitomized the Texan persona. Logan, had a demure, relaxed calm that was reflective of the laid-back tropical feel in Florida. Both were successful, though, because they were recruited from the local population. "The idea was," said Dick Wrublik, "that you could talk as a local corporation rather than a 'foreign' corporation."

A local company versus a national conglomerate was an important distinction for people in the towns across America. In the early years, when U-Haul opened up companies around the country, the competition capitalized on an associative model of local, hometown dealers loosely unified, as opposed to U-Haul, which was based in Portland. "Your local competitors," said Hap Carty, "the one advantage they had on us, they were hooked up. You know in zoning, you know they knew the local policemen, the mayor and all this kind of stuff. That's why Sam developed the policy of hiring a local person to be president of a local company."

The result then was not U-Haul of America, but U-Haul of Florida or U-Haul of Texas—the best of both worlds. It provided centralized leadership from Portland directing a focused campaign for the success of all the rental companies, which then encouraged cooperation locally and nationally. As Ron Frank put it, "The people working in Seattle were just as focused as the people in Miami," whereas the competition was disorganized. "George Nelson [of Nationwide]," said Ron Frank, "had a much bigger operation in Miami than we had. But he had, as I recall, Florida as his franchise. And somebody else would have Georgia and Mississippi. So if the guy in Charlotte, North Carolina didn't like George Nelson, well he wouldn't send George's trailers back or George Nelson wouldn't send him trailers."

* * *

DESPITE THE HARD work and nature of opening dealers [essentially sales], many young men in U-Haul desired to be AFMs. The field rigs of the AFMs were often their home. Some men were on the road for weeks or months at a time. They kept a cot in the van and slept there. This was probably done because of Bob Clarke's review of hotels in *Management Bulletin 25* in which he wrote, "Hotels in almost every city are either very expensive or very dirty and full of vermin." His endorsement of restaurants was not much better: "[And] it is my conclusion that about one out of ten middle class restaurants in the country is a fit place to eat . . . the food doesn't taste good, the dishes aren't clean, the coffee is bad and generally, the service is equally bad." Clark had a good basis for his judgments. The bulletin points out that his territory "could loosely be defined as the continental United States of America."

Clark thought restaurants were "a supplemental form of life support." Instead he suggested that AFMs "stock about a three-day supply of bread, sandwich meat, cheese, cookies and fresh fruit to assemble at least one, preferably two roadside meals a day."

It was a policy that was born out of necessity. The do-it-yourself tradition is born out of making do with what one has, generally with a severely constrained budget. This requires stripping things to their bare necessities, using only that which is needed to get the job done. Excessive spending took money away from the operations needed to build and market trailers. Clark's bulletin became something of a sacred text for future AFMs, who would endure life on the road.

AFMs were the ones nearest to the action, opening dealers throughout the country, something akin to trailblazers. Perhaps they felt a certain thrill on the road, or perhaps the road helped them discover themselves "at the dividing line between the East of my youth and the West of my future," as Kerouac's Sal Paradise saw himself. But unlike Sal, these men saw purpose and a clear road to the "West of their future."

7

THE SECRETS OF SUCCESS

BY 1955, THE Fleet Owner Program was running smoothly. Trailers were being sold faster than Dick Wrublik could order them. The company was moving in the right direction—up, and literally bursting at the seams. There was no room for all the employees at the ARCOA headquarters anymore. A sign of such upward mobility was the company's move from Foster Road to Hawthorne Avenue in Portland. The move was not without some controversy, according to Tom O'Donnell, then the office manager. "[T]hey had all this wartime housing in different areas around," said O'Donnell. "They [U-Haul] went out and bought an old commissary from one of these housing developments, and they cut it in half and they put a foundation in there for the basement, and then they brought this old building in there in halves. I guess the neighbors found out about it before they got quite that far and they raised a ruckus, and so everyone was going out, going around the neighborhood trying to tell them that it was going to be pretty nice when it was finished. They finally got enough to agree because it came in."

The new location posed a further, albeit cosmetic, problem, "When we first moved in, we were spacing the desks trying to make it look not too bare," said O'Donnell. "We had a problem of making it look like it was a growing operation."

If there was a theme to 1955, it was graduation. The company had graduated to the top of the class in trailer rentals, and Sam himself graduated from the Northwestern College of Law at the top of his class. The legal knowledge he garnered would help him with the U-Haul System's next step: the Certified Average Registration Plan (CARP). A growing company, such as U-Haul, in a rapidly expanding industry, such as the one-way trailer rental business, required an adept knowledge of laws from state to state, especially licensing regulations. It required a political touch and constant contact with local and state politicians.

"The average person in politics now can't hold a candle, in my view, to the kind of people we had in our cities and our state and in our government in Washington, DC at that time," said Hap Carty.

Hap remembered being in the Northeast in the '50s, and learning that Connecticut was about to ban the types of hitches U-Haul used. Not really sure about due process or the mechanics of the political machine, Hap took a drive down to Connecticut. "I thought, well I'll talk to the state engineer," said Hap. "I didn't know what in the hell the state engineer was but it had the best title."

Upon his arrival, Hap met with Wilbur Cross Jr., the State Engineer. Hap made the case for reusable hitches rather than frame hitches: they could serve more people, they cost less, some people would not be able to afford frame hitches and, therefore, would be unable to move using a trailer. "Well, he picked up on that right away," said Hap, "and he asked me to come back on another day. And he took me down to a legislative committee that was considering this thing. And I didn't know it at the time, but he was the guy that they [the groups proposing the legislation] got to propose outlawing bumper hitches. He told the committee, 'I think you should listen to this young man. I think he knows more than I do on this subject.'" And with that, the legislation disappeared.

Remember Sam's remark in *You and Me:* "I think I hit the trailer rental industry at an opportune moment." The type of politician described by Hap in this era proved to be a vital ally for the rental business in general, not just U-Haul. U-Haul had a special relationship with legislators that proved to be beneficial. It was not backroom lobbying; it was purely good customer service. Legislators, councilmen and judges used U-Haul trailers, and their personal experience was so positive that they worked to help U-Haul as best they could when it came to zoning, and in turn U-Haul helped them.

Hap's efforts reflected a proactive approach in the field of legislative affairs that differed from the U-Haul Company's competitors: "When the association of the trailer people was set up, I was the U-Haul representative for the fourteen northeastern states, and I have yet to meet anybody that ever showed up from their outfit for any problem or legislation or anything at any time."

Active lobbying on the part of U-Haul helped the company overcome the greatest legal hurdle to the trailer rental industry: licensing.

Dreisbach saw how, even in the early days, licensing was a problem. "There was a Washington state police officer, who would sit across the state lines and wait for our trailers to come across," he said. States charged license fees which paid for roads; trailers sent one way from another state, and rented locally for an extended period of time, were subject to penalties for not having a license for the state they were presently in. U-Haul needed to address this issue soon, since technically their business model was illegal, and further expansion might bring more headaches.

The man spearheading the licensing effort was Jack Lorentz. Lorentz, who was hired in 1953, graduated from the University of Santa Clara Law School in 1950. His tenure at U-Haul was both highly respected and highly effective. For many years, Lorentz *was* the Legal Department. To the men in the field, he was their best friend. "He was a lot more than what a lawyer is in most people's minds," said Hap of Lorentz. "He gave tremendous support to people like myself who were operating in the field. If you got a lawsuit, if you had an accident, if you had a zoning problem, you could always depend on Jack. We picked up the phone, and called him and could generally forget about it."

His expertise was called upon when licensing became a primary concern at the main offices of ARCOA. In 1955, Lorentz and Sam published a pamphlet entitled, *We're Asking for It!* It was an important piece necessary for the survival of the trailer-rental business. "What we fear," the pamphlet read, "is that proposed legislation may ignore us, or may be interpreted as applying to us when it was really written for somebody else."

The primary dilemma was classification. Classification allowed states to establish an equitable contribution to highway maintenance. But no one knew exactly what a trailer was in terms of classification. Was it a vehicle or an accessory? Or both? States could classify trailers in a variety of ways, which would cripple the rental industry as it tried to stay current with forty-eight different statutes. "We honestly don't know what our share of highway upkeep should be," the pamphlet explained. *We're Asking for It!* classified trailers as "auto accessories."

Because trailers weighed less than cars, had half as many wheels and were "responsible for less than half the wear and tear to the highway," this classification seemed justified. Furthermore, towing a trailer caused a car to consume more gas, twenty to forty percent more: "Naturally, this add[ed] to the state's revenue by way of the gasoline tax." So whatever state a trailer was in benefited indirectly.

Once the classification of trailers was established, a fair measure for assessing fees was needed—the "it" the pamphlet asked for. Trailers passing through a state were rarely stopped, according to the pamphlet. "Only when the trailer's destination [was] reached [did] the real problem arise." This problem forced companies to practice "selective renting," which sent trailers with out-of-state plates only on one-way, out-of-state rentals. This, of course, was impractical and led to a backup of trailers in certain areas. The other option aside from selective renting was a sneaky, less ethical loophole: purchasing licenses from a state with the lowest fees.

To avoid these two unenviable options for the rental companies, a Massachusetts plan, Certified Average Registration Plan [CARP] became the national standard. CARP "provide[d] that trailer rental companies[. . .]register and pay taxes on the average number of trailers operating within and through the state." U-Haul would "furnish carefully computed records of the average number of trailers in any state during any week of the year." The final certification of these numbers rested with each state's secretary of state. The company did all the work; the state had only to approve the numbers.

After the per-state traffic percentage was established, the company then purchased licenses proportionate to the percentages for each state through which their trailers passed, so that "full interstate and intrastate reciprocity [was] granted."

"I was kind of scared when I first read the thing," said Hap Carty. "I figured the next bureaucrat I ran into, wherever I was at, was going to hit me over the head." Fortunately for Hap, the man who stepped to the forefront of selling this plan to the motor vehicle departments of the various states, was the company's number-one salesman, Sam Shoen.

Sam, and many times Anna Mary, crisscrossed the country, hosting salty-dog breakfasts. "And I mean it was salty in those days," said Logan Frank, "plenty of vodka. We'd make a big old pot of salty dogs and they'd lap them up." Behind the scenes, Jack Lorentz worked tirelessly to make sure rental company managers stayed on top of license purchasing.

"We tried to be fair with everybody," said Hap. "I think that we bought 105 percent of as many licenses as we really needed. In dealing with us, I think they got the sense that we were pretty damn straight shooters."

"I have heard," said Pat Crahan, currently the head of Legislative Affairs at U-Haul, "and I'm not sure if this is true or not, but that there was one state that didn't require a trailer license at all, and Sam sent them money anyway. And he said, 'It's fair that you get this money because if you had a license plate, you should get this money. So here's money for you.' He was very fair."

In the end, CARP caught on with the states in part because of the initiative the company showed in trying to resolve the issue before it ever got out of hand. Moreover, U-Haul endeavored to solve the issue in a manner that satisfied each state's demands, not just the demands of rental companies.

* * *

AS 1955 BECAME 1956, U-Haul was on the cusp of making giant strides forward. Major changes to trailers, rental policies and marketing were in the works, all designed to accommodate the customer and better market the product, in order to pull farther ahead in the trailer business.

U-Haul and its network of dealers and rental companies had grown significantly, enough to warrant the creation of five regions headed up by regional directors. Hap Carty handled the northeast; Warren Albers, the midwest; Bert Miller, the southern states; Vern Olson, the West Coast; and Norm Dacus, the southeastern states. It relieved L.S. of some travel; instead, he would rely on quarterly meetings with the regional directors who managed things on the micro level.

U-Haul introduced the Emergency Aid Program to provide customers with roadside assistance if problems occurred with the trailer, a service renters appreciated. The competition did not offer such assistance. In an article in *U-Haul News*, the program was hailed as a success: "Discussions with prospective customers show that they are often surprised U-Haul can make such an offer, (after all . . . what other company can?)."

Other changes that took place across the System were direct results of the pamphlet *We're Asking for It!* The second half of the pamphlet addressed an important facet of the new business, and one that U-Haul considered a strength when compared to the competition—quality of equipment and service. The company at this time ordered trailers faster than they could be built. In 1954, a metal stamping plant was set up in Willow Grove, Pennsylvania. Initially it was built to stamp out a new trailer, the "Loadmaster," but it soon became a crucial part of a new type of manufacturing for U-Haul.

AS THE SYSTEM expanded, communication was imperative. Since 1953, U-Haul published *U-Haul News,* a monthly periodical designed to feature stories highlighting dealer innovation, moments when fieldmen and dealers went the extra mile for customers. It had "Sam's Corner," a small spot at the end of the issue where Sam would impart bits of wisdom to his readers. Often it featured a cartoon by Ray Robbins that reinforced whatever policy that particular issue was trying to drive home to the dealers.

Robbins, who had left U-Haul to serve in the military, returned to Portland in 1956 to find U-Haul a remarkably changed organization. In particular, marketing was a greatly expanded department. Commerce at that time demanded it because companies understood "the growing power of advertising in American life." Consider that BBD&O, a major marketing company at the time, saw its billings go from $40 million in 1945 to $235 million by 1960. Yale historian David Potter explains, "that in a culture of so many choices, as America was in the fifties, it was inevitable that advertising would come to play an increasingly important role."

The new ad men were a new type of hero in the American landscape. Movies like *The Hucksters* starring Clark Gable and Deborah Kerr glamorized the profession, and showed its potential dark side. The field was anything but stylish. It involved "long hours, high turnover, [and] bred ulcers and heart attacks. Studies comparing the health of men in advertising with that of executives in other professions showed them to be in consistently poorer health than their peers."

These were hardly appealing prospects for the new person running the Advertising Department, Duane Swanson, but he avoided those pitfalls, and launched the dynamic marketing machine that would help make U-Haul a household name.

Swanson was a graphic design major at Lewis and Clark College. His physical stature matches his artistic talent. He is a giant of a man, who today, even in retirement, is the captain of the fire department in his hometown. When he came to U-Haul, he was initially rebuffed. "[T]hey knew that I still had a month of school— of college—to finish and they needed somebody right away, so they hired somebody else," he said. Still, Swanson insisted on doing the interview. Two weeks later, U-Haul called and offered him a job because "the first guy they hired didn't work out," said Swanson.

One of the biggest marketing successes for U-Haul outside of the trailers was advertising in the Yellow Pages. To underscore the importance of the Yellow Pages, at every town Sam stopped in, he would check to make sure the Yellow Pages advertisement for U-Haul was correct. Pat Crahan remembered one time when the advertisement was not correct. "He was upset about the Yellow Pages, the way the Yellow Pages were worded. And he said, 'This is wrong, wrong, wrong, wrong,' and you know, all the Yellow Pages are wrong the whole city directory is wrong, and on and on and on. And it was like . . . my fault, and I had only been there a little while, and if you know anything about Yellow Pages you have to do them a year in advance. So I said, 'Mr. Shoen I don't know too much about the company, but I can't go around and pick up all the phone books in Oklahoma City and issue new ones. Whatever it is we've got to live with it.' So he said, 'Okay, take down this telegram. So I take down this telegram to Mr. Tom O'Donnell, 'Don't ever do this again blah, blah, blah,' and he dictated this letter to me. Then he said, 'Get Tom O'Donnell on the phone.' So we got him on the telephone. So we sent him a letter, and a telegram, and got him on the telephone. So I learned quite a bit about the Yellow Pages, and we never had a mistake in the Yellow Pages ever again."

Staying on top of this campaign was not easy. According to Swanson, "Every week there were certain directories that closed. And you had to make different ads for them. The printing process in those days was quite antiquated compared to today. Whenever you printed an ad, you had to put it on a copper plate on a wood block, and mail that to the publisher. It wasn't done with computers."

The Yellow Pages were utilized by many other companies, including the U-Haul Company's competitors. There were stark differences between the competition's and the U-Haul Company's advertisements, though: "Our brand name and our design and our sales points that we included in the advertisement," Swanson recalled as key differences. "And we could list several dealers. Our competition was made up of independent dealers. They may have

had bigger lots with more equipment, but we had more convenient service by using the service stations scattered around."

Mike Morelli affirmed this convenience in the sheer number of
dealers, "People used to come in and ask me if I'd take their trailer
[from a competitor]. I'd say, 'It's not my company.' And the person
would say, 'But I can't find a dealer.'"

There was yet another bonus for the U-Haul dealers in the
advertisements. "We would list the dealer's name and address in our
ad, and that was a benefit to him. It didn't cost him anything," said
Swanson. This underscores Wrublik's point that the Fleet Owner
Program allowed ARCOA and the U-Haul companies of the various states to devote their revenue to Yellow Pages advertising. This
kept them from having to charge the dealers for advertising,
which meant one less stress among the many that Ron Frank
noted.

Swanson set to work revamping the U-Haul Company's biggest
marketing tool, the trailers themselves. Like other U-Haul System
members, Swanson went into the field, worked at dealerships and
took note of displays. He soon helped devise display manuals for
dealers. But he noticed something else about the trailers. "After I
had been there awhile," explained Swanson, "I could see the trailers were a yellow-orange with black stenciling. And they were
pretty crude. I thought the orange and the black were just too
heavy looking."

He also brought an end to the days of stenciling "U-Haul" onto
the trailers. "That technique was pretty crude," he said. "If you've
ever painted with a stencil, and you've painted more than ten
times with a stencil, the stencil fills up; the paint fills up the holes.
So it starts looking sloppier and sloppier, or the stencils slip." The
alternative? Decals.

The U-Haul trailer was in for a major overhaul. Ten years after
danger orange graced a U-Haul trailer, the fleet was ready for a
makeover. The new colors were not guaranteed to be orange
either. "[Duane Swanson] and I were painting, and he would tell
me what color to paint it, and I'd go out and paint it blue or green
or orange," said Phil Schnee, who was back from Boston and

assisting Swanson with the experiments in color change. "For a very short time we were looking at *anything* but yellow," he said.

Eventually the color scheme settled upon was a red–orange on the bottom and white for the top. Swanson justified his choice by saying, "I thought the tops should be a white color so the trailer would look lighter weight and also cut down the overall appearance of the height so that it would look more streamlined." The logo on the top remained orange until the trailers began having aluminum tops. "When they used aluminum tops, then I recommended they change to it a dark blue so it had more contrast against the aluminum. Orange against the aluminum looks dull. On pure white, it was okay."

The switch was not welcomed by all. Even in a young company like U-Haul that was only ten years old, many of the veteran System members were resistant to the change. "I think that was my first ulcer with the company: trying to develop that program," said Swanson.

But Ron Frank loved the new look: "I think changing the paint scheme from the black and orange to the white and orange was something that was significant because it presented a bright new image to the public. The black and the orange didn't look well when compared to the white and the orange. It just look[ed] better."

Additionally, the US trailer was put aside. The US trailer was unique in that it used curved plywood paneling to create the perception that the trailer was highly aerodynamic. It resembled a Roman chariot, something that could have been raced in *Ben-Hur,* rather than move possessions. To the builders, it was a thorn in their side. "That trailer was just a lot of extra work," said Dale Webber. "Because for the wood panels you took a four by eight sheet of plywood and you cut that out. And you didn't have a circular saw. You used a skill saw. I don't think we ever got above [producing] ten or twelve trailers a week. It was just so much work. We built those in Des Moines," Webber explained, "and it just took so much time to bend those railings. You're doing it all by hand. You bent that whole rail with a torch."

By August 1956, U-Haul trailers had a totally new look. The newly redesigned UV trailer rolled off the assembly line at the Chicago plant. It had half a dozen new features. It is easy to imagine the competition cringing. While they fought to keep up with repairs on their equipment, U-Haul introduced a trailer that had Duraply (paper finish for the plywood sides); redesigned fenders; a redesigned trailer tongue to "take more wear and tear"; Goodyear Hi-Miler, six-ply tubeless tires—*U-Haul News* proclaimed, "U-Haul will be the first to use it exclusively"; revised taillight and turn-signal wiring; a new rear bumper; and, most importantly, a solid Duraply rear door that replaced the canvas rear covering and would "insur[e] weather-tight coverage of customer's cargo."

The new trailers looked sharp and robust. The grief Duane Swanson endured while making the transition was clearly worth it. "There's always resistance when people meet change," he said, "but the program proved so good that it really enriched the fleet. It cleaned up the fleet. It made it look contemporary." Swanson's foresight and deep consideration for each choice was his strength as the head of the U-Haul Company's advertising. His first major initiative was a fantastic success and would propel him into bigger, more successful campaigns in the coming years.

TWO THINGS ARE often credited for the U-Haul Company's triumph over National and Nationwide: marketing and a superior product, which in turn led to customer satisfaction—the ultimate benchmark of success. Yet there is one department that often goes unnoticed: the Traffic Department. Without Traffic there would have been no vigilant distribution of trailers throughout the country. They would have gotten stuck in Southern California and Florida. And with the trailers stuck, they would not have moved, and therefore, would have failed as marketing devices. Duane Swanson's efforts would have been for naught.

Helen Shoen moved to Florida in 1952 when her husband Kermit was sent to handle field duties for that state. What he found, according to her, were "trailers located in Miami [that] had been there for so long that weeds were growing up through the floorboards." Even in 1952, Helen Shoen witnessed what would be the bane of U-Haul Company's business in Florida: more people were moving into the state than were moving out. As Americans flocked to the Sunshine State, U-Haul trailers piled up, languishing on dealers' lots.

"I remember one time," recalled Logan Frank, "Nationwide and National kept cutting our price[s]. So I took 150 trailers in Miami, put 'em on the lot and I put a big sign up saying, '$2 Anywhere in the Northeast United States.' This was an anomaly. We didn't do this all the time. Well, Mr. Shoen told me he wanted me to rent these trailers north." This promotion demonstrates the measures Sam would approve to get trailers moving out of Florida.

"I know for a fact that the only efficient way of moving a trailer or a truck is by customer," said Hap. "And it causes a lot of mental anguish to people that don't comprehend the concept because if you build a demand slightly beyond your supply, it happens. If you build a demand slightly below your supply, you take it in the neck."

Sam preferred to keep trailers moving by rentals. The alternative, transport on trucks, was a last resort. "Sam was always against this, but he didn't prohibit it: moving trailers [by truck] from one place to another," said Ralph Shivers. If a trailer was rented and moved to a new location, the trailer made money during its transfer. But if trailers had to be shipped to a location in need of them, U-Haul had to pay for the shipping. Hence, the Traffic Department evolved during the mid '50s in order to keep trailers from piling up in the areas of the country experiencing population booms.

"It was a jigsaw puzzle that was fun to work with," said Shivers. "Every week you would have the information available. You have every area in the country, how many trailers are there, how many of each kind of trailer was there." The department's goal was to keep the trailers out of what Shivers called "sumps." "If it ends up in a sump, which was like Florida, Southern California or Arizona, we were being put out of business. Our revenue was going to go down."

From the ARCOA office in Portland, Shivers and Pauline Kidweiller would track traffic every week and recommend rate changes for dealers in the sumps. But they were only recommendations. Rental company managers were more aware of the situation in their areas than people in Portland. The recommendations did not always work, though, since the recommendations meant slashing prices to rent a trailer in order to send it out of a sump, and dealers' commissions were impacted. Meanwhile, trailers piled up and the company as a whole was losing money.

Shivers explained the solution, "[W]e didn't want these trailers that were in Area A, so to speak, going to Area X, because they weren't going to earn any money. There were just too damn many trailers there for what was coming in. This is where surcharges came in." The word *surcharge* struck fear into the hearts of rental company managers.

On the surface, the surcharge might appear to have been a severe handicap to dealers. The surcharge was determined by ARCOA in Portland. It was applied to rentals going to sump areas. Dealers then charged the customer the surcharge on top of the one-way rate. The surcharge went directly to ARCOA. The dealer received no cut from the surcharge. Occasionally, they would lose customers because of the surcharge.

Shivers sometimes had to play the role of bad guy. "I got into wrestling matches with my brother [Ken]," said Shivers. "They wanted to rent a trailer to Florida. It wasn't in the organization's interest to do that. You know, they're on the local scene and they didn't see it as readily; on occasion, I wasn't real popular with people. They couldn't always take the easy rental because the price was such that the customer wouldn't pay it. And well, all right, the customer won't pay it 'cause that guy in Phoenix or Portland or wherever [we] happened to be at the time was putting the surcharge on. On the other hand if I had let them all go, pretty soon they wouldn't have had any trailers!"

Jim Shaw, who was in charge of Southern California, a sump, was not a fan of surcharges and recalled, "I don't care how much explanation you gave, dealers had their opinions, and they had a right to their opinions. They were *independent* dealers." Shaw lobbied Portland as best he could on the dealers' behalf. "Anybody's ear I could get, I bent."

Part of the problem was in meeting local demand. Although surcharges did not affect local rentals directly, they did so indirectly through the amount of equipment available in the sumps.

"While we originally had a pileup," said Shaw, "I thought that we reached a point where we were not contributing to the System and really needed more equipment. I had the people, the prospective customers, the service stations—everything we needed to get into it more and more. They still had surcharges on to me, and I didn't like it much. I wanted more equipment."

Dale Green, who worked under Shaw at this time, remembered the dealer backlash. "Normally, they didn't like it because they felt like they were losing revenue, losing a rental because some of the surcharges were pretty stiff," said Green. "So they thought they were losing business and commissions on it, sales they could've had. Normally they didn't like it but they accepted it because it changed from month to month."

Like in any good business, though, the Traffic Department worked with other System members to facilitate an effective surcharge policy. "We talked to rental company presidents and regional directors on a regular basis trying to discuss what was appropriate and what was not appropriate," said Shivers.

Surcharges became an effective tactic in moving past Nationwide and National. "Part of this surcharge deal would be to discourage our equipment from going to Florida," said Shivers, "and hopefully send the customer to Nationwide and let their trailer go to Florida and stack up down there. It was a twofold deal: keep us from having all of our equipment sitting down there and not making any money, and to nail old Nationwide and National and get them to take that rental to Florida and get sucked into the deal."

Dale Green witnessed the success of surcharges for U-Haul overall. "Any competition, when U-Haul put a surcharge on, our equipment going to [the sump] would slow down so that our competition would keep sending trailers and trucks into there if they had them and have the same situation we did, which is surplus," he said.

This tactic seemed somewhat odd, even counter to what U-Haul impressed on its dealers through the Sandy McTavish cartoon strip, in which Sandy played the dealer who "never let a customer get away." Shivers, though, was resigned to losing those customers, "I don't know what [the competition] did. I don't think they were nearly as into it as we were. We don't want that trailer in Florida. We'll let that trailer go to Colorado, or Iowa, or someplace where it's going to earn some bucks. If it goes to Florida, we're screwed. Ultimately, it was win-win for everybody. By not letting that one trailer go to a sump, the company was able get twenty rentals from it."

"Rent them where they'd rent them back. That was our goal," quipped Hap.

Working in the Traffic Department sometimes made Shivers privy, albeit unknowingly, to top secret, national-security issues. Shivers became suspicious when he noticed some odd changes to traffic for North Dakota. "You couldn't keep a trailer in North Dakota for anything," he explained. "I mean you'd have the state of North Dakota, and maybe there were thirty thousand trailers [in the System] and you couldn't keep twenty-five in the whole damn state. Nobody's going to North Dakota. All of a sudden we got trailers coming out the ying-yang in North Dakota. Now what in the hell is going on? We really didn't know. But we all of a sudden—you nearly had surcharges going into North Dakota. We finally found out what it was . . . missile silos. The Cold War. They were building missile silos to dump 'em on the Soviet Union. It took a lot of people to put those doggone things in and they took U-Haul trailers."

Ralph Shivers valued his years in the Traffic Department more so than his years in the field as rental company president and as one of the early fieldmen. He said, "That probably wasn't my strong suit. I was adequate at it, but I wasn't among the elite." He was one of those early trainees who worked in Oakland for Dale Graves and Dale Webber. But one of the great signs of success is for a person to know their strengths and their weaknesses, and put themselves in a position where they can bring to the company their strongest attributes. Shivers discovered his calling after returning from Pennsylvania as a rental company president. His calling was in the Traffic Department.

8

THE WOMEN OF U-HAUL

THE ROLE ANNA Mary Carty Shoen played in U-Haul is described as invaluable by all those who knew her or were involved in the U-Haul System from 1945–1964. "She was the strength behind Sam Shoen," remembered Dreisbach. Women played key roles in the growth of the one-way trailer rental business. Whether it was working at the ARCOA headquarters in Portland, or the wives of marketing company presidents working as unpaid secretaries, or dealers' wives who encouraged their husbands to be dealers in the first place, women helped U-Haul become what it is today.

Logan Frank remembered the first U-Haul dealer in Wichita Falls, Texas. "I knew Mr. Davis and his wife. In 1951 he received this trailer and an information packet," which Logan saw later when he was working for U-Haul. "I should have got that from him, but anyway it said, 'Congratulations, you are a now a U-Haul dealer. Here is your first trailer. Rent it for fifty dollars and send me half the money,' or something like that. I remember Mr. Davis said, 'I wasn't interested in that trailer' but his wife said, 'I'll take it.'"

Many visionary and determined women saw the potential in the trailer-rental business, where perhaps their husbands did not. Imagine being a service station owner and receiving a trailer one day, and then being told how to care for it and rent it. At best, it would appear to be just another aggravation. At worst, the service station owner might see it as a scam, and forget about the trailer or use it for storage. Yet people like Mrs. Davis in Wichita Falls saw the potential in this new venture or were at least aware enough to see that, in the interim, the trailer business was something that could nicely supplement the family income.

"We were at a time in the evolution of service stations, where many of them were run by a man and his wife," explained Hap Carty. It was quite fitting that the base of the nationwide network of one-way U-Haul dealerships succeeded due to the teamwork of a husband and wife. Hap said the marriage between his sister and Sam was "a match made in heaven." The same could be said about the company those two built and the service stations.

Phil Schnee recalled seeing Anna Mary at work during one of Sam's trips to California. "She worked right along with Sam. They traveled quite a bit together. I recall, as a field rep when I was in Southern California, that Sam and Anna Mary came into a dealership that I was servicing. Sam was out working with me a little bit, and she was in doing the books. She was fairly active with the company at that time."

Hap added, "The places where the wife worked in the business made the best dealers. One time, a friend of mine, a man named Vin Kiley [Hap's confidant, special-projects manager; a man who, according to Hap, "had the guts, the instincts and the perseverance to get the job done."], did a survey of the top one hundred dealers in the country, and in ninety-some of them, the wife worked in the business."

Historian James Patterson writes, "The rise in female employment was one of the most powerful demographic trends of the postwar era." Women were just starting to enter the workplace en masse. World War II offered them the chance to get out of the home and earn substantial money in some challenging jobs. The end of the war is associated with a decline in women in the workplace, but as Patterson notes, "While demobilization adversely affected many women workers, it did not stop the steadily increasing desire of women, especially middle-aged and married women, to test the marketplace." Many women joined the ranks of U-Haul, employed either full time or as the wives of U-Haul System members. Sometimes the wives' work was unpaid and done out of love for the family they cared for at home and the one they found in U-Haul. It was a partnership.

It took a special type of woman to endure the job the husband worked. Often, the wife would be pressed into service to help work on trailers. In the office, women were just as versatile as their male counterparts, if not more so. Their responsibilities in the company sent them to work in all departments. One thing is certain, from the dealers to the top of ARCOA, from day one until the present, U-Haul relied on women at all levels and in all roles to help expand the company in the first twenty years. Without them, the company would not have grown nearly as quickly, if at all.

"[ABOUT] THE TIME you get a baby almost walking, they would move us," said Mary Shivers, Ralph Shivers' wife. She cringed when Sam was in town. "I used to hate to see him come, because he could convince me to do anything. I mean he would just sit and talk and the next thing, I was ready to pack and haul kids all over the country in a trailer or whatever he came up with. And I'd always say, 'Wait 'till I see Sam, I'm going to tell him.' And he'd come, and I'd agree."

Mary Shivers had seen Sam when she was a student at Marylhurst. Mary had no idea that roughly seven years later, in 1951, she would become a part of the U-Haul family, and in some cases serve informally as one of the first "fieldmen." The day after Mary and Ralph Shivers were married, Sam sent the two out on a six-month road trip opening dealers and doing repair work. "Mary would fix the safety pins [which were used to wire the taillights of the trailer to the car]," said Ralph. The car they drove had no air conditioning so they drove at night. Mary did not know how to drive a manual transmission; if Ralph needed to sleep, he would set the car in motion for a short distance, and then the two would switch seats.

At one point, it looked as if the newlyweds would not even make it back to Portland. "We got into Casper, Wyoming, and the checks came but nobody knew about U-Haul so nobody cashed the damn things," said Ralph. "We stayed in the hotel for two or three days because nobody would cash the check. I remember sitting out on a riverbank, and we had some crackers and grapes and Mary thought it would be her last meal. We were out of money."

Helen Shoen experienced a similar induction into U-Haul. The family was sent to Florida, and they embarked on a twenty-nine-day trip, which involved visiting dealers along the way. At one stop in Knoxville, Tennessee, she and Kermit were to recover a horse trailer. "The agent told us, 'You better take firearms if you're going in the backcountry.' I wouldn't let [Kermit] go alone, especially after he told us that."

The excursion into the backcountry went off without incident, though they did not find the trailer. "It was a new experience for me. I was upset because I thought someone would come after us with a double-barrel[ed] shotgun," said Helen.

Outside of work, they had to entertain the children too. "There were times, when we didn't get into town until 9:30 or so," Helen explained. "Hopefully we would get a place where there was a park or a playground for the kids so they could get out and get a little exercise. Kerm would come back and check us out, and sometimes he wouldn't be through, and we'd wind up at a service station, which is really fun and games because it's not a place for little kids."

When they arrived in Florida, finding a home was difficult; they lived in a hotel for a time. "We were glad to find a place to live. We needed to get our first-grader back in school; however, I tutored her en route," Helen recalled. Their new home had an office, too, which was housed in "a small front bedroom." Helen served in the informal role of office manager. "I worked and checked to see where the equipment was, and what was coming in," she said. "I had a list of all the dealers and answered all the calls. I would call each and every dealer and find out what equipment they had, and see what they might need. Then if someone needed a trailer, I could tell him where it was and he could go get it." The home also received calls from customers "[t]o find out where to drop off the equipment."

ANOTHER FLORIDA RENTAL company manager ran his company in the same manner as Kermit and Helen Shoen did. Logan Frank and his wife, Dee, were another husband–and–wife team whose work strengthened the dealer network in Florida. Dee Frank said she took over as her husband's assistant primarily because of clutter. "Shortly after he became what they called rental company manager then, L.S. decided he didn't need an office, or anybody to open the mail or do anything," said Dee. "What [Logan] did was stack it all in a corner for six months. And of course who can you hire off the street to take care of that? So I got the job."

Dee also assisted with trailer distribution and getting the trailers out of the sumps. "We were constantly moving the trailers the best we could as far north as we could on transports," she said, "which I did also, when they had an extra field rig. That was part of my duties of running the office." She loaded them herself as well. Dealers were duly impressed. "I got a lot of double looks," she said.

In 1963, when the Franks relocated to Arizona, Dee proved invaluable to Logan. "There was a brief period in Tucson, where I had a problem with asthma," explained Logan. "And for about six months, I really had a problem. And finally it went away. So Dee, she fixed the wires, and aired the tires."

"And I wasn't on the payroll," interjected Dee. "We'd had the one child at that time, and she had to go with us in the truck, in a cradle, because Logan was not physically able, at that time, to do the manual labor. So he did the paperwork and I did the manual labor."

On top of the day-to-day responsibilities, Dee brought the dealers closer together at Logan's dealer meetings. Logan encouraged dealers to bring their wives to these events. "I had mostly gotten to know the wives of a lot of them when I'd be on these rigs delivering trailers. So a lot of them I had already known when we had these meetings," recalled Dee. "But that was a good place to get acquainted with the wives, and if the wives were happy with them being dealers then the men were happy." At the meetings she "include[d] them in everything. Don't let anybody—any wife be secluded [sic]." So while Logan built the *esprit de corps* among the dealers, Dee worked to create camaraderie among the wives.

Logan and Dee were both aware of the need to not exhibit any type of favoritism. Dee was the boss's wife. Other people in the office might have resented any favoritism shown toward Dee, or worse, would have disrupted office work by keeping her at a distance in order to avoid her "telling on them." "When I first started traveling with him from marketing company to marketing company," said Dee, "it never failed that he would make an example of me on something. Something I might not have done right just to show that I had no favor. I didn't get any favors."

"It was done in a tactful way," explained Logan.

"Of course it was. But it helped me because then the rest of the people in the office looked at me as just one of them," said Dee. "And I made a point of never, ever telling Logan anything that went on there unless it was an absolute necessity—theft or something like that. I wanted them to feel like I was just one of them."

"I told Dee, 'Gossip—I don't want to hear it,'" said Logan. "And they knew—they weren't afraid to talk to Dee because they knew she wouldn't run back over to me and tell me something trivial. I wouldn't hear it."

ELAINE DESHONG PARLAYED her unpaid time working for her husband into a legacy at U-Haul. Her husband, Harry DeShong Sr., was a fixture in the Arizona-Nevada rental company. She did a number of things to ensure that company's success. "Harry was bitten by the concept of U-Haul. So I was too. Wives either were or weren't U-Haul," Elaine said.

When Sam visited, she usually picked him up at the airport. She respected him for his energy and thrift. "You respected the man for what he was building and [had] helped build," she said. "He always wanted to stay at the YMCA. I'd pick him up and he'd say 'You gotta take me to the YMCA.'" She, instead, had him stay at her home.

Other times, she answered calls from panicked dealers complaining, "'A guy just came in and started working on trailers.' And I'd say, 'What's he look like?' And they'd describe Sam to a tee, and I just said, 'Let him go. He owns the company,'" recalled DeShong.

Her home was no refuge from the world of U-Haul. "Fieldmen had a key to my house," she recalled. The number for the U-Haul company was her home phone, which meant she took on the unofficial role of customer service representative for Harry's company. In doing so, she grew concerned that the customers lacked immediate satisfactory feedback.

By 1963, Elaine DeShong was establishing what would eventually become the U-Haul Company's official Customer Service office. "I was appalled by the poor customer service," she said. "No one would answer their letters." That same year, "U-Haul became the only rental company to have a hotline. It was a red phone," she said. "We had to develop a hotline list of dealers and field personnel."

At the heart of DeShong's crusade was compassion. "Moving is one of the five most stressful experiences in a person's life, right up there with death and divorce," she said. "The more personal your relationship is with the customers during this traumatic event, the more service you provide to them."

ANOTHER INTERESTING COUPLE was Jim and Vivian Shaw. As the company grew, it was not unusual for members of the System to marry one another. (Jerry Ayres is credited with the first U-Haul "merger," in 1955.) But when Vivian came to work at U-Haul in 1954, she and Jim were not yet married. Jim had not started working for U-Haul yet. Her husband at the time was ill, and her daughter, Mary Jane, was a special-needs child who attended a private school. Vivian took a job in the Data Processing Department. "I was opening dealer Monday Reports with a hand letter opener," she remembered.

Margaret Carty and Dorothy Davis were early office workers at the Foster Road office. As other women entered the System, the early women of ARCOA were revered in a manner not unlike the AFMs' reverence for the first fieldmen. One of the grand dames of the early ARCOA years, and far beyond, would be Vivian Shaw.

Vivian Shaw had a tenacity that was unrivaled by many men within the company. She was never afraid to speak her mind. Such tenacity was needed for women at this time in American history, as they forged ahead into the working world. "I felt I had to work better and longer than anybody else, and put more effort into my job than anybody else in order to get ahead," she said. "But I just did it naturally. I was taught that when I was growing up by my parents. 'Nobody's going to hand you a golden platter, Viv. You have to work hard for it.' That's the way I was raised."

Office work was time consuming and complex. "We had quite a Data Processing Department," explained Vivian. "We had three Remington Rand keypunch machines: one sorter, one merger and a tab machine. The programs were prewired and the heavy units we had to set into the tab machine were real heavy, and then of course we took those round-hole Remington Rand punch cards from the basement, and we had to carry those big cases up. We developed a lot of muscle."

The machines were problematic, though, as Vivian described: "They printed the checks, and we had to make sure everything balanced. That led to 'Checkmate Charlie' later on in the program. I designed that because they ran the checks through the computer too often and they were wrong and they had to be redone. Something was always wrong. The month was wrong. And so, Checkmate Charlie was a procedure, where each step you take, you check certain things, and you wait till you get to the bottom and then you're okay. Then you can go ahead and run the checks. It was a checklist that we checked the balances of everything: our journal vouchers and different things like that had to balance before we could print the check." In a company that prided itself as being a sound investment for dealers and fleet owners, Vivian Shaw's

Checkmate Charlie ensured that dealer and fleet owner checks were distributed on time, lessening tension between ARCOA and the people who needed their money.

Despite annoyances with the Remington Rand machine, Vivian enjoyed her job. "I never once got up in the morning and said, 'Oh, I hate to go to work,'" she said. She and Ethel Bible made their jobs fun, sometimes to Tom O'Donnell's chagrin. "We used to drive poor Tom crazy, I'm sure, because we were quite wild, but we did a good job," remembered Vivian. "They had several different machines, and they would get the machines going, the Remington Rand data-processing machines there, and they'd provide a different rhythm. So we would constantly kind of bee-bop around there with the different rhythms, and Tom would walk around the corner and his poor face would just drop."

The work they did was serious, though, and they knew it. Dick Wrublik relied on them to compile fleet information to better administer the Fleet Owner Program. According to Vivian, Wrublik galvanized the women. "Dick Wrublik was very, very good at keeping people informed and explaining to them what they were doing," she said. "He never tried to keep anything from us. You know, 'Do your job and don't pay any attention to what it is. Just do what we tell you to do.' He wasn't that kind of guy."

Her first encounter with Sam was when his temper flared. Even he was aware how quickly he could spark, but Anna Mary would usually touch his arm and say, "Hush, Sam," and he would instantly calm down. On the day Vivian first met Sam, though, Anna Mary was not around. "He was giving Tom O'Donnell hell, right in the middle of the office. Here was this guy just screaming at the top of his lungs, and I thought 'Who is that uncouth man?' Then I found out he owned the operation."

Her subsequent dealings with Sam, though, were much more enriching. He held meetings at the ARCOA building regularly for all the System members. "He would talk to the whole group," said Shaw. "He was a very dynamic person. Of course everyone was terribly frightened of him. Well, at least us peons were. He was a hard driver but that's why the business is so successful today."

Jacque Hedwall, who came to work at U-Haul in 1959, and whose experience spans six decades in the System, remembered these meetings. "He would have meetings after work. He wanted your input," she recalled. "He would tell you what was on his mind at that particular time and then he wanted input. But he would also make you a part of where he wanted to go with the company. He inspired me, for one thing. I could sit there for hours and listen to him talk, if nothing else. But not only that, he made you feel like you were a part of everything that was going on. And that what you had to say and what you were doing was important."

As her job evolved, Vivian Shaw had to deal more frequently with dealers, who were almost all men. "Some of it was pretty rough. They would have questions about their Monday Report, and weren't satisfied by the girls who took care of it. So I would step in."

She was not meek, and certainly did not know the meaning of giving in. "I grew up with seven brothers," she said. "And boy they taught me a lot. And I also grew up with two nephews. And we fought. I'm telling you. We would get into fistfights. We would draw an imaginary line across the grass. 'Don't step over that line,' and one of us would step over it. Boy, then the fists started flying."

Lessons like that helped her hold her own. Her toughness did not go unnoticed either. "Ken Shivers and [I] butted heads a few times," remembered Vivian. "Sam was there when we butted heads, and Sam would complement me, 'You know how to handle them, don't you Viv?' I said, 'Yeah, I do.' He said, 'Good work.'"

She pushed her subordinates to look beyond their current job. "I would talk to them, if I had a bunch of gals around me," said Vivian, "and I would say, 'Now, okay, who wants my job?' Nobody would answer. I'd say, 'Oh c'mon gals, who wants my job? If none of you want my job, you might as well leave because that's what you should be shooting for is my job.'"

It worked. "I had some great gals who worked for me," she said.

Vivian eventually assumed a motherly role to her female coworkers. "I felt that. I felt that there were a lot of women who looked up to me," she remembered. But when asked about the toughest part of her job, she became somber and then replied in subdued tone, "When someone would come to me with an emotional problem. That was hard to know what to do."

The role Vivian Shaw played at the ARCOA offices was immeasurable. As Vivian recalled, "They were mostly women in the corporate headquarters." A strong spirit such as Vivian Shaw galvanized the women. At the same time, she earned the respect of the men in the office with her own work.

MANY OF THE departments at ARCOA during this time were made up of one man. Ralph Shivers was referred to as *the* Traffic Department just as Lorentz was *the* Legal Department and Swanson was *the* Advertising Department. They were "the high muckamucks," according to Vivian Shaw. "It was endearing," she said.

The "high muckamucks" did not hide away in their offices. "[There was an] open door policy," remembered Jacque Hedwall. "It was like, Jack Lorentz, he ran a department. Jerry Ayres ran a department. Ralph Shivers ran a department. You could walk in anytime you wanted. It was just the way it was. They didn't stand out as being any better than anyone else. Each of us felt that we were a part of that company, and a part of the decision-making process, just with direct input."

There was always someone from the pool of females working at ARCOA assisting the department heads. No one was specifically relegated to assisting in one department. Vacations or illnesses meant spot substitutions. The women had to be prepared to work for any department, which meant they had to be as aware of each department's function as the top men in ARCOA. "I worked for Jerry Ayres in Repair Processing Statements. I would do work for Jack Lorentz. I'd even work over at Duane Swanson's area. And we had a typing pool at the time, so if they got behind, if someone was gone, I'd go back to the typing pool," recalled Hedwall.

For his part, Shivers was quick to pass off full credit for the role the Traffic Department played in U-Haul. He had someone else helping him—Pauline Kidweiller. "She was a partner with me," said Shivers. She called rental company managers, negotiated rates and

soothed dealer concerns over surcharges. "She was just a phe-
nomenally competent individual," continued Shivers. "Like I say,
we went through two, three or four guys, you know, out of college
who had good degrees. They didn't have a clue. It took me going
through two or three of them before I figured out, *she knows.*"
Eventually the two of them were seen as a powerful office duo,
whose teamwork powered the Traffic Department, which was so
instrumental in helping U–Haul outpace the competition.

Women were often called on to help at state fairs or trade
shows, too. "You go into the recreational shows and . . . you'd set
up a booth and you'd have a display," said Jacque Hedwall. "A lot
of times we just set up a booth to obtain dealers. So you'd give out
guides to people going by. Let 'em know it's not a franchise so you
didn't have to buy into it to be a U–Haul dealer. It was a way to
get U–Haul dealers, visit with people, answer any questions. We'd
have a schedule because the shows would be open from maybe ten
in the morning to nine [or] ten at night. So you'd take maybe four
hours in the morning." Hedwall typified the versatility of the
women at ARCOA. They had to know the ins and outs of the
company in order to represent U–Haul in a professional and
informed manner.

DEE FRANK OFTEN worked as a U–Haul barker at state fairs. "I
hated that job," said Dee. "I'm not an extrovert in that case. And I
soon had to learn to be one. Logan would just drop me off and say,
'See ya in five hours.'"

"I'd say, 'Get that microphone out there, and drag some people
in here,'" said Logan of his instructions to Dee.

Dee was up to the challenge to "get [customers] in just to get
them to recognize U–Haul. We'd give them these little paper trailers, and explain to them about the rentals," she said. "I don't know
if they were receptive or just laughed at me," she joked. "No, they
were interested."

The U–Haul displays that Dee managed often had covered
areas, which proved to be valuable marketing hooks: "Interesting

thing about state fairs, wherever we lived, Florida, Phoenix, anytime there was a state fair, they'd have good weather until that week. It rained the whole time."

THE TRAILER BUSINESS, like most businesses in the '50s, was dominated by men, but the women of U-Haul took every opportunity to achieve the standards of their male counterparts. More often than not they succeeded. This was most evident in the story of Edith Johns as detailed in a *U-Haul News* article, "Who Said It's a Man's World?" Mrs. Johns entered the service station business with her husband George in 1958. Not long after, however, George passed away. Mrs. Johns took over the Mobil station and U-Haul dealership. "Almost everyone likes to see a person overcome handicaps and go on to win," explained the article. "Mrs. Johns' customers were no exception. They encouraged her—and brought her more business. In short, they liked her spirit. And they made it known at the cash register." Eventually she would be a AAA dealer, the highest level of dealer certification. Her case proves that the rigors of U-Haul demanded a person (man or woman) with unusual drive and focus on service.

WORKING FOR U-HAUL, whether in the field or at ARCOA, put a certain strain on families. Even Anna Mary confided to Ann Lorentz that it was hard to "be both mother and father" to the six kids who now filled the Shoen home. Sam was often on the road trying to get rental companies set up with good managers and fieldmen, or out east helping Safford or Hap develop new products. Anna Mary's comments were not said out of frustration nor were they meant to disparage Sam. "She wasn't putting him down," insisted Lorentz. "I never heard her put him down. She wasn't like that."

Martin Carty concurred. "Anna Mary was as supportive as one could be of the business, also knowing that she had the children to raise," he said. "But as in any family I'm sure—well I know there were times where I'm sure it would be nice if Sam were home a bit more. But Anna Mary and Sam dealt with that very well."

The lifestyle took its toll on everyone. A U-Haul wife was married to the company, too. "Sometimes these men forgot they had wives at home who really stood up for them," said Vivian Shaw in a somber tone. "There are a lot of good wives in U-Haul who stick up for their husbands, and stay up all night if their husbands are out working late."

Ron Frank has such a wife, Miriam, and he certainly never forgot the effort she gave to build their family despite the long hours he worked. He arrived early to his shop every day. "I physically worked eight hours with the crew. When they put their eight hours in, at 3:30, they walked out the door. I then would do all the cleanup. I'd put all the tools away, put all the supplies up," said Ron. "Many times Miriam and the three kids would come down to the shop; we didn't live that far away. I'd have a piece of plywood on a couple sawhorses. Miriam would bring dinner down, and she and the three kids and I would sit around the plywood table, and we'd talk about the day. How was school? How was this? Do all the family communicating. She then would gather up all the dirty dishes, the food and the three kids, and go home, and I'd work a couple more hours. Many days, that was the routine."

Hap, too, knew how lucky he was to have another coworker at home: his wife Toni. "Best unpaid worker U-Haul ever had," he quipped.

"The other thing I liked about the company when I started: It was kind of family oriented," said Jerry Ayres. "It was all a private company. It's family oriented. You knew everybody in the office. It was all friends in this thing." What kept any strain from becoming too overwhelming was that familial feel within the company. Family was clearly important to U-Haul. Many of the first System members were related to Sam or Anna Mary. The people in the System at this time looked out for one another, as family does.

Jacque Hedwall saw that family atmosphere as a catalyst for building a stronger company: "That was one thing that was always good about U-Haul anyway. Everything was a team effort. That's what I meant by saying it was like family. Everybody cared about the other person. You did whatever it took to get the job done. If you were done with your work, you'd go over here and over there or over here."

This sense of teamwork probably caused Dick Wrublik to be stretched a bit too thin. But it was the shared sense of family within the company and the wives that prevented a potential burnout. At one point, Sam insisted that Wrublik go to law school on top of his duties at ARCOA. The Fleet Owner Program still required constant care. So after work, Wrublik attended law classes and studied when he was at home. Suzanne Wrublik, his wife, was under tremendous strain at home. Anna Mary, with whom Suzanne was close, insisted that Sam get Wrublik out of law school, in order for him to be home more with Suzanne. Sam obliged.

This was not uncommon. "We knew everybody's husband and wives and their kids and their parents. It was a real family environment, a lot of fun at picnic time," said Vivian Shaw. "It was a good feeling. It felt like you had some security."

Company picnics were another part of U-Haul that helped bring System members closer together. Everyone enjoyed their jobs, but these annual events, along with the Christmas party, were a pleasant bonus for System members, a nice getaway with friends away from the office. The first picnics, small functions where they had only to push a few picnic tables together, were held at Mount Hood. Jerry Ayres remembered them with a great deal of fondness: "The company picnics were a small group of people, so you knew everybody. You had the gang together so you knew what everybody was doing."

Later, as the company grew, the picnics were moved to Lake Merwin in Washington. "We would have these men who would barbeque on these big, big, *big* grills, you know, the half-chickens," remembered Ann Lorentz. "Then they would have trailers that would have a lot of beer and other food."

IN OCTOBER 1956, Anna Mary suffered a heart attack. Sam kept her alive with artificial respiration and eventually she began breathing on her own and regained consciousness. The shock of the attack was downplayed by Anna Mary's cardiologist, who had monitored her condition for years. He "very convincingly told us that this was unlikely to happen again for another thirty-five years," Sam wrote in a letter to his children in 1957. "He said the worst mistake we could make would be to change our way of living a full life."

Anna Mary took the doctor's advice, according to Ann Lorentz. "We were going to go to a function for Marylhurst College. I think it was a dinner dance," she said. At a cocktail party before the alumni function, Anna Mary, while talking to Ann Lorentz about the heart attack, appeared unwilling to live life timidly. "She said, 'Well I've decided that I just can't lead my life that way. I'm just going to go on the way I normally do.'"

"I stayed pretty close to Portland for the ensuing months and made only short trips," wrote Sam. "However, as the months went by without mishap or apparent signs of a change in her heart, I developed unwarranted confidence." The routine of life's daily business soon returned to the Shoen household by May 1957. Anna Mary would soon celebrate her thirty-fifth birthday. In the meantime she busied herself with purchasing dishes for the church, gardening and preparing a benefit dinner for the Little League baseball group to be held the next day.

Ann Lorentz had given birth earlier in the month, and when she and Jack came home from the hospital they received a phone call. "We were in the bedroom because I remember him sitting down on the bed and saying, 'Oh, no! Anna Mary,'" said Ann, "and right away I knew something had happened to her, you knew before he got off the phone."

On the night of May 4, 1957, Sam slipped into bed quietly in order not to startle a sleeping Anna Mary. She awoke and said, "Oh my God, Sam, you frightened me!" Those were her last words. She fell into a coma, and although Sam did everything to revive her, she never regained consciousness. Sam called for Sammy and Mike, his two oldest children, who called Dr. Todd, the family doctor. Soon Dr. Haney, her cardiologist, and Father Walsh arrived. Despite their efforts, Anna Mary received the Last Rites, and shortly afterward, despite many attempts to revive her, Anna Mary Carty Shoen passed away. "She died quickly and, I believe, without pain," Sam wrote.

Her death devastated and angered Sam. "From a mortal's viewpoint it is terribly unfair. However, I realize that she would not have concurred, in this view. Her faith in God, her Catholic beliefs were as real as the rising of the Sun [sic]," he lamented.

Anna Mary left behind six children. Paul was the youngest, barely able to walk. She was buried in Ridgefield, Washington, in a family plot. Sam built a beautiful monument near her grave. It features a statue of the Virgin Mary keeping watch over the cemetery. Flowers surround it. For the rest of her life, her mother had a mass said daily for Anna Mary. The nuns of Marylhurst were grief-stricken as well. And Sam was inconsolable.

Those who knew Sam attested that he was never the same person; even in running U-Haul he was a changed man. The letter he wrote to their children two days later, in some ways, foretold this: "Time will dull my memory and my life may again appear to be a happy one. Nevertheless, it can never be the same. Everything on earth that is mine was conceived and built with her: you children, my Catholic faith, my legal education, and the U-Haul business. Wherever I turn or go or do, I must acknowledge her hand. What I am, what I possess, I owe in great part to her. I never knew true happiness until our marriage. Perhaps I will not know it again on this earth."

"YOUR JOY IS your sorrow unmasked." This begins "On Joy and Sorrow," a poem in Kahlil Gibran's classic, *The Prophet*, popular in America during the 1960s. The book attempts to demystify the seeming randomness of life. Sam was a fan of *The Prophet*. In *You and Me,* he reprinted one of the poems from the book, "On Children," above a picture of his family. "On Joy and Sorrow" continues, "And the selfsame well from which your laughter rises was oftentimes filled with your tears. / And how else can it be? / The deeper that sorrow carves into your being, the more joy you can contain."

Although Sam was devastated by the loss of Anna Mary, his sorrow was eventually filled by the joy of a new wife and five new children. On September 12, 1958, Sam remarried. His bride was Suzanne Gilbaugh. Her parents were neighbors of Sam and Anna Mary. Pictures from that day show that she reinvigorated Sam. He looked tan, rested and a bright smile covered his face—a remarkable contrast to the haggard widower photographed with his children just months after Anna Mary's death. But on September 12, Sam looked like a man who had rediscovered his purpose in life.

Suzanne shared many qualities with Anna Mary; she was highly intelligent, but she was without a doubt her own person. When she met Sam she was in graduate school in North Carolina, receiving a master's degree in public health. She had an innate maternal nature that assisted her in adjusting to her new family. Her entrance into the Shoen home was not an enviable one, considering she would become a stepmother to six children, without ever having been a mother herself. But as Elaine DeShong recalled, "Sue worked very, very hard to help Sam, and be a mother for all those kids." She endeavored to make sure the kids were raised as Anna Mary had wanted, a quality Anna Mary's parents admired in Suzanne.

She was immediately well liked by the family, both Shoens and Cartys. "She's a good friend of mine, and my whole family. She's about the only person that I've ever met that got along with all the Cartys," Hap said with a good natured laugh. He then paused, and his tone became much more serious. "She was like an angel to my parents. You know she had six kids to raise there, plus she [eventually] had her own kids. She was, absolutely, a real blessing to my parents, and of course everybody in the family picked up on that."

Suzanne had to jump right into the duties of a company wife. She had to travel with Sam to meetings with the motor vehicle departments of various states, where they continued the tradition of salty-dog breakfasts. As someone noted, "Her honeymoon, in part, involved accompanying L.S. on a business meeting in San Francisco." She also arranged company social functions in her home.

Eventually she and Sam would have five children. But as many people who knew her attested, she had, and continues to have, a deep pride in all the children she helped raise. Her entry into the world of U-Haul allowed Sam to refocus himself, and lead the company into the next decade, one that featured major innovations and change for the company and the young industry. Without Suzanne, Sam's return and the course of the company might have been severely altered for the worse. She was the embodiment of the prototypical U-Haul wife: supportive; unselfish yet self-sufficient; she shared the vision of what U-Haul could be with her husband.

"On Joy and Sorrow" continues, "And is not the lute that soothes your spirit, the very wood that was hollowed by knives?" At a time when Sam's life had been hollowed with knives, Suzanne was the lute that soothed his spirit.

AN INDUSTRY
(1960–1964)

9

TAKING THE LEAD

THE POSITION OF ARCOA office manager implied that the person serving in that position was the de facto boss. Sam's traveling was due in part to his disdain for the tedium of office life. Instead, vital yet often mundane work such as dealer communications and responding to claims fell to the office manager. "Sam didn't like that, so he was happy to get someone to take it off his back," said longtime office manager, Tom O'Donnell.

Dick Wrublik remembered the early years when Charles Dreisbach ran the office. "[U]ntil [Sam] started the management program, he was gone on the road. And [Dreisbach] was running the company from the office."

In the first year after Anna Mary's death, Sam's involvement with U-Haul was spotty. Prior to meeting Suzanne Gilbaugh, Sam went to Europe to convalesce and recover from the loss of his wife. The task of running the company once again fell to the office manager, Tom O'Donnell. During Sam's recuperation, O'Donnell and the ARCOA staff took steps to propel U-Haul far ahead of the competition.

* * *

WHEN HE FIRST interviewed with U-Haul, it didn't seem like Tom O'Donnell would fit with the company. Fixing trailers was not what he envisioned himself doing with his college degree. Sam considered the point and said, "The person that is running the office right now is Charlie Dreisbach. He's going to be going into the seminary after the summer, in the fall. Do you think you'd be interested in that?"

O'Donnell was interested. "So a couple days later he called me and said, 'Are you ready to go to work? What we're doing is—all these people that are coming in, they're all starting at the bottom. And they are starting in the shop and going through all the phases of trailer building. I think everyone should do that. Do you have any objections to starting now and going through that this summer and then come in and take over when Charlie leaves[?]' So I said, 'No. I'll go through that."

When he took over as office manager, though, he had to teach himself. "I never really got much instruction from Sam on how to do anything," said O'Donnell. He looked through old files and figured out the daily operations of his job, primarily claims. "Practically everything was denied," he said. "[The customers] were always wrong. Well I tried that for a couple of weeks and I couldn't stomach that sort of thing. So I started a little more lenient program, and I'd go talk to Sam and say, 'This is the wrong approach, Sam.' Because to build up an organization, you've got to treat people right. And he agreed to that."

As he put in time with U-Haul, O'Donnell gained a reputation for being a strong, decisive leader. He was not as demonstrative as Sam, and did his work quietly behind the scenes. Sam worked diligently, put in long hours and traveled the country. In order for that to happen, O'Donnell made sure things ran smoothly in Portland. Dealer correspondence was cut down with the expanded role of the *U-Haul News,* where memos to dealers were disseminated en masse, as opposed to time-consuming letters to individual dealers regarding the same topic. O'Donnell was certainly ready for the new role he took on in 1957.

The years of 1957–1960 were critical for the company. Sam's habit of not giving too much instruction on a position's duties, in favor of letting the person determine their job's description, paid off. The major issue facing U-Haul was the unprecedented growth brought about by the success of the Fleet Owner Program. "They kept us growing and growing because they were adding more trailers. And we got more fleet owners, more employees, more of everything. More payroll," said O'Donnell. The year-end charts for 1957 showed a company on the rise: 22,000 trailers in the fleet (there were still three months to go, too), an estimated $6,000,000 in rentals and a dealer network of 3,100.

The sheer volume of documentation was overwhelming. As such, problems arose in getting fleet owners' checks out on time, and holding dealers to timely submission of their reports was also difficult. These difficulties convinced O'Donnell that U-Haul needed to buy higher-powered IBM computers.

Before purchasing the computers, issues with the dealers needed resolution but with a personal touch, requiring lots of man-hours, to ensure there were no oversights. The biggest headaches with dealer relations involved the timeliness of dealer reports. Some were not mailed on time, and those that were encountered a lag time before they were fully processed. "If [the dealers] were in a bind they'd just tap into that money and [not] report [it]," said O'Donnell. "So we had dealers who hadn't reported for several months who owed us five to six hundred dollars. And we were losing money hand over fist on that thing."

O'Donnell remembered that Sam, who was about to leave for Europe, was reluctant to change anything that might adversely effect dealer relations. "Sam always looked at it from the dealers' standpoint," he said. "If the dealer kind of goofed up, well, don't bear down on him too much because he didn't want to lose the dealer. That's the guy that's really producing the money for us. This is true. But we were losing a bundle. And that really bugged me, since the first time I got in and saw it going on."

A change in policy was suggested: one late report and that dealer could no longer simply deduct his commission. "[W]e would compute their commission," explained O'Donnell, "and at the end of the month we would send them a dealer check, similar to the fleet owner check." Additionally, delinquent dealers' commissions would be reduced from 25 percent one way and 40 percent local to 20 percent one way and 30 percent local. If they were on time, there was no punitive cost incurred by the dealer. The commission remained the same.

"I don't think we can do that, but go ahead," Sam said in response to the new plan.

"As long as it worked, he didn't care," said O'Donnell, "but if it didn't work, then that was a dumb thing to do."

For the new plan to work, "we had to get the field behind us," said O'Donnell. "So, we decided to hold a convention. Sam was gone, so we were going to hold a ring-dinger."

All the AFMs and rental company managers were summoned to Portland. True to the unspoken policy in U-Haul at the time, all those invited brought their wives as well. "It didn't cost people anything," said O'Donnell. "They could sit down and talk about their complaints. We met with them, and kind of outlined the idea and then tried to get some ideas from them that we could incorporate in this so they'd be a part of the program."

The new policy was a success, in no small part due to the people in the field, who had been appropriately consulted. They would meet with dealers who were irritated over the new policy. O'Donnell used incentives to ease the transition. "[T]hose dealers that report on time, we will take that money that was forfeited by delinquent dealers and we will put that money in a trailer fleet. We will have dealer trailer fleets. So that kind of softened the blow," said O'Donnell. If nothing else it proved to the dealers that the new policy was done only to encourage and reward responsible dealers, not line the pockets of ARCOA. The money would help build more fleets. In the grand scheme of things, everyone's best interests were served.

The new policy required more computation and better record keeping on ARCOA's part. If ARCOA intended to make the dealers more responsible and timely, the accounting in Portland had to be timely as well. Additionally, the Fleet Owner Program required specialized record keeping, and O'Donnell recognized that all of this slowed down operations. More importantly, he wanted to make sure fleet owners received their money on time. After all, they were financing the growing company.

"You see," he explained, "it was really a problem to get the fleet-owner checks out on time. They were due to be out the twentieth of every month and we would send a whole list of all the activity of all the trailers in the fleet. Where they went, the dealers they were rented from, the dealers that they were rented to, the amount of money, local or one-way, *a big sheet* [emphasis added]."

At that time, computers were mammoth machines. The one U-Haul eventually purchased had to be housed in a separate building, away from the Hawthorne headquarters. "We didn't have the air conditioning [the computer needed]. We kept it downtown," said O'Donnell. In terms of what the machine's capabilities were: "[I]t probably didn't do half as much as a desk computer does today."

The computer system was up and running by 1960, and was turning out "all the dealer statements and checks, and fleet owner statements and checks, and payroll checks, and all the different reports that we needed and could get were available." As to whether Sam knew about it, O'Donnell was not sure, "He was removed from it." In the end it helped streamline service for U-Haul and its dealers and fleet owners.

O'Donnell is one of the names that always comes up when speaking to U-Haul System members. His work and diligence helped the company avoid many logistical headaches.

"THERE'S ANOTHER GUY that I want to be sure that you mention—Tom Safford," said Hap Carty. "He was kind of like Sam only his talent was not business, although he was no dummy, but he was gifted big time in getting a production line set up, in getting a product designed, that type of thing. Working in the practical. He kept us in business with his talent."

Tom Safford's ingenuity and mechanical skills solved many problems U-Haul had with its equipment, and he even pitched in with art work, designing the first "Sammy" U-Haul logo.

Safford was an enigmatic character. "Tom Safford used to come and go from the company," said Ron Green. "I don't think he was ever off the payroll. He used to leave us and come back; leave us and come back." Sam put up with these leaves of absence, and did not resent or distrust Safford when he took them; Sam and Safford worked too well together.

"He would integrate or fit with Sam just like a glove," said Ralph Shivers, "because Sam had absolute faith in him. Tom was just flat-out creative." Sam knew what a unique individual like Safford meant to the company, because unique individuals like Safford were essential in other companies' success stories.

"He *was* engineering," said Ron Green. "He was it. Almost everything, he designed or built. The guy ... he's a genius."

An interesting parallel to Safford would be Charles Kettering of General Motors. David Halberstam describes Kettering as "the resident technical genius" at GM. He points out that Kettering's "inventions were critical to the company's, indeed the industry's, success." He created the automobile self-starter (a key rather than a crank), heaters for cars and all-purpose Duco paint, which cut the drying time on cars from seventeen to three days. Coincidently, Kettering's work in 1946–49 benefited U-Haul. As Sam observed in *You and Me,* "During the '20s and '30s, few automobiles were adequate to tow a trailer." In 1947, Kettering presented plans for a new high-compression engine that gave cars more power, which could be used to pull the trailers U-Haul had just begun to build.

Safford's contribution to U-Haul was similar. He worked on practical solutions to problems that plagued the company and its customers. An unassuming man, Safford might have echoed Charles Kettering on any type of praise for his innovation: "I'm a wrench-and-pliers man."

"Safford was absolutely a lifesaver in the product end of our business," Hap said. "Sam and Safford worked up this product guide of standard parts and I think that dated clear back to when Sam bought those oddball trailers." From there, Hap clicks off a list of Safford's inventions and skills: he could hook up a trailer in one minute; invented wire hookups, the surge brake, latches for trailer doors; designed a paint system for trailers; built the first press shop at Willow Grove. "I didn't know what a six-hundred-ton press was," remembered Hap. Safford did, and it was instrumental to the self-sufficient production of U-Haul trailers.

"Tom created what we called a universal hitch," said Ralph Shivers, "that would fit maybe eighty to eighty-five percent of all the doggone vehicles." It was Safford's first major contribution to the company. Sam had made a hitch in the early days, but Safford's proved more versatile and effective. Ralph Shivers recalled that every year, "a car would come out with a different bumper and Tom would solve the problem. We must have had fifteen or twenty different styles of hitches. You'd have a dealer with several trailers and you'd need—to fit all the cars—twenty different hitches. Well, it just wasn't practical."

Consequently, a new hitch was needed for every new car. Tom was up for the task, and amazed Hap. "A new car would come out with a new bumper and Tom would design a hitch for it in twenty-four hours," he said.

Safford created the Loadmaster Trailer, the first all-metal trailer. His work on the Loadmaster came, in part, because of pileups in sumps. Sam, as has been mentioned, hated paying to haul trailers, primarily because it was not economical to pay for a sizable chunk of space on a transport truck for a relatively small number of trailers. "I think Sam and Safford thought the one way of solving the imbalance of equipment was to build a trailer that could be knocked down and shipped," said Hap. "Safford and Sam worked on developing this trailer called the Loadmaster Trailer: all steel. It was a knockdown trailer. The tongue would come off. The canvas cover came off. The undercarriage came off, and you threw it inside the trailer box and you'd ship it." But the trailers were often damaged. "You had to have parts shipped in, and it was getting to be bodywork," said Don Shivers. Another problem arose: assembly and disassembly were not always as efficient as the designer had said. This discrepancy between Safford's assembly time and other people's was indicative of Tom's mechanical dexterity.

Dick Wrublik, who admired Tom Safford tremendously, did have one small, good-natured bone to pick. "One of the things I didn't trust him on is that whenever he would tell me how long it would take to build anything, I had to double it," said Wrublik. "Because what he would do, he would go out there and lay everything out and learn how to do it really well, and he would hit hard for whatever it is, and then use that time. Well, you had to buy the parts. You had to line it up. You had to do all these other things. And one person can't work at that speed for forty hours a week, you follow me, eight hours a day. So you couldn't make that goal. We couldn't rely on [his test run], not the fact that he didn't do it . . . he did . . . but because nobody could keep it up."

Hap and Safford worked well together, which Sam appreciated. Perhaps the reason they worked well together was because Hap understood Safford's talent and the temperament that went with it. "He was a designer, not an engineer," explained Hap. "Engineers are misunderstood. A good engineer is a person who can take the work of somebody like Tom Safford and get a crude working model, and get it in production without screwing up the concept. Engineers are not designers. Hiring an engineer to do a design job is like hiring me to be the center of the Phoenix Suns."

More than anything else, Safford was beloved by the people who knew him. Helen Shoen explained the exuberance her children had when Safford was in town, and she probably captured the sentiment of all his colleagues: "[M]y kids just adored him. One time at Christmas, he made the picture of Sputnik with the Christmas tree on our big sliding glass window when we were in California, and that's when Sputnik first came out, so that gives you an idea of the date [1956]. And he had a little, tiny, bright pink Thunderbird . . . and the kids would see that pink car and run out lickety-split. They just really thought that he was really very special, and [he] was very special." He was known as "T-Bird Tom" because of the pink Thunderbird, his calling card of sorts.

He was a loner, but in no way disagreeable or surly. Dick Wrublik comprehended Safford's disposition. "He was an excellent staff person," explained Wrublik. "He wanted to really do a job and test it, which is what you need. I mean, you don't want somebody to do it sloppy when safety is involved. He tended to want to work alone. He didn't want to work with other people. He didn't want to manage other people. He didn't like to come up and say, 'Joe, do this, do this.' He tended to do it himself. 'Because,' he said, 'by the time you explain it to them and do it, you can do it faster.'"

ABOUT THIS TIME, the American Dream received a makeover. It no longer mimicked Horatio Alger novels, where his hero Ragged Dick is the beneficiary of the classic, rags-to-riches story. According to historian James Patterson, "few sensible citizens had ever imagined that." They still did believe in the American Dream, but it was not "defined by the belief that hard work would enable a person to rise in society and that children would do better in life than [their] parents."

A product of this revamped American Dream was a new type of worker who dominated the industrial scene of the United States, "the Hydrocarbon Man." For nearly a century, in what was known as the coal age, workers clawed to scrape out a meager living. But Hydrocarbon Man "was the beneficiary of his own labor." He built items that were affordable to nearly every consumer in the United States, regardless of class.

Naohiro Amaya, a Japanese intellectual, was fond of saying that had Karl Marx seen the living conditions of workers in the 1950s, his writing might have changed drastically. The new laborer owned his home and a car, and had a degree of comfort traditionally attained by only the affluent or social climbers. This success was a new source of pride for workers who loved their work, but never sought executive advancement. These workers created a new gentility within the blue-collar workforce. In turn, lifelong laborers prospered in an expanding middle class.

"I mean, for a person to be around all these years, you'd think I'd be some manager in some shop. That's not me though," said John Zuransky, who works for U-Haul at Boston Trailer. "I'm a worker. Not necessarily working the same thing over and over and over.

You'd get bored to death. But I do like work. I'm not the bossy type or the type who's made to be a manager."

Don Shivers echoed Zuransky's words. "I'm not good at running people," he said. "I was good in the shop. I know what to do, but I don't like pushing people. I'm not a good manager. Not because of knowledge. It was just because I don't move people."

The men behind the scenes in the plants were quiet, unassuming and often overly modest about their work. Toward the end of his interview, Don Shivers smiled and said, "I'll bet you most of the people you interview will be on the other end [the field], which is the more interesting end." Yet, just as it took a special person to be an AFM, it required a different type of person to devote themselves to the plant work, but it was no less exciting. Big changes were taking place in the plants.

Zuransky, who had been with U-Haul since 1958, retired in October 2006. He walks the shop, proud of each piece of shop equipment he made, and proud of every truck he built or trailer he repaired. In some ways, he has a childlike awe about him even after all the years he had worked for U-Haul. This is his first impression of the company: "My parents' house was right across the street [from Boston Trailer] and that's where I lived. So I was pretty fascinated. I was always watching—I was still going to high school at the time—I was always watching them when I got home because I was fascinated with the way they built the trailers and what was going on there. So I got to know Hap. And I graduated in '58, so I said, 'Well this is real convenient, right across the street I might as well go work there.'"

Zuransky was a prize hire and someone Hap had been watching for a while. "I knew John when he was a little boy," Hap said. "He lived right across the street. His old man had his ass pushing a wheelbarrow or something, working all the time. This kid was always working—busy. I don't remember how in the hell we hired him. But I know that we wanted to hire him from the time he was a little kid because he's just a hardworking guy."

When Zuransky signed on, though, the center of East Coast manufacturing was no longer in Boston. The manufacturing plant was still in Dedham, but the high demand for trailers up and down the East Coast forced U-Haul to move major industrial work to a central location. Zuransky recalled just how in demand the trailers were. "I was amazed, on weekends, to see the trailers leave the shop unpainted," he said. "That's how much of a demand the trailers were in. Then they'd come back from the local rental [on] Monday and they'd stencil them and paint them. That amazed me." Willow Grove, located just outside of Philadelphia, took over as the major manufacturing site for trailers on the East Coast.

"Willow Grove was a different market," explained Hap. "The Fleet Owner Program had developed where we had quite a few available sources wanting to buy equipment. And the magnitude of the market, we didn't know what it was, but it was a hell of a lot bigger than we were. And the Boston Trailer plant was not a big plant. The trailers we built in Boston were primarily designed to be made out of barstock, you know, channel iron, angle iron, bolts; weld them together." A bigger plant with metal-stamping presses and the capacity to crank out the constantly evolving trailers was needed.

In 1954, the Willow Grove site had been purchased. Initially, it was a gamble for Sam, though. "I knew of an instance where he mortgaged himself to the hilt, his home and everything, to build up what was then called the Willow Grove Plant—an old conglomeration of buildings that we kind of put together and made work," remembered Jim Shaw.

While it allowed for expanded production, the floor space was still insufficient. "We added on a whole bunch of floor space," explained Hap. "We actually built around some of the machinery we brought in. Safford bought that big [metal-stamping] press at an auction."

That big metal-stamping press ushered in a new era for U-Haul manufacturing. "In 1956, [Willow Grove] built six thousand trailers," said Hap. "We stamped out the parts for those trailers, and we also stamped out most of the repair parts for the whole U-Haul System." The new equipment allowed the company to manufacture its own parts, another addition to the do-it-yourself work ethic that had helped build U-Haul.

* * *

THE SUCCESS OF many companies at this time rested on their capability of producing the necessary materials for manufacturing the product. Not the least of these successful companies was Levitt and Sons. Their product: a suburban community. Levittown was the brainchild of William Levitt, who mass-produced quality, affordable housing for many Americans. (Ralph and Mary Shivers actually lived in one of "Levitt's towns.") Paul Goldberg of the *New York Times* said that Levitt's homes "turned the single detached single-family home from a distant dream to a real possibility for thousands of middle-class American families." Like U-Haul, Levitt had a system of mass production that required efficiency. Anything that slowed them down was a catastrophic blow to production and thus the service they offered their clients was slowed. To prevent this, they "made their own nails, buying thirteen nail-making machines and a great supply of scrap iron; they made their own cement; and they even bought their own lumber, buying thousands of acres of timberland in Oregon and building a mill there." It was another reaffirmation that the do-it-yourself work ethic permeated all facets of U.S. prosperity in postwar America.

WILLOW GROVE SOON improved efficiency Systemwide and sped up production. "Once they got Willow Grove going they'd stamp parts and then ship parts to all the little plants," explained Don Shivers. "Tongue parts and actually frame parts, too. They would stamp out the pieces, then they would come to the place, and you'd put them on the jig and weld them together."

"You couldn't afford to have a stamping plant for every shop," said Hap. "But you could afford to have one stamping plant, and then ship parts to Boston. The first distribution truck we had, I started that thing myself. I bought the biggest most powerful Kenworth made. I scheduled delivery a year ahead of time. 'That truck will be in your shop next March the second. And the cutoff date for your order is this, and everything you order will be in that truck and there will be no backorders.'That was killing us, the backorders. So if a guy had to backorder all the time, he'd order three times as much as he'd need."

Some of Hap's people from Boston came down to help. Ron Green was one. Not long after Ron arrived, he had a visitor from Portland—his brother Dale. "I went to visit him for a summer," said Dale. "Between my junior and senior year in high school, I stayed there." He was quickly introduced to the world of U-Haul.

"While he was there of course," said Ron of Dale, "Sam heard he was coming into town and he said, 'Well, we'll put him to work then.' And he did. When it came time for him to go back for his senior year, Dale decided to stay in Pennsylvania and go to school there. So we called my parents and they said, 'Well, as long as you make sure he goes to school, all right.'"

"I really didn't have a lot of social time," said Dale. "I was working after school. If I remember right, it was something like, 3:00 or 3:30 to 10:00, Monday through Friday." Dale's shift allowed him to see the various jobs at the plant. "Night shift, they'd have four to six guys doing some extra work and keep the production going. I was doing some painting on some miscellaneous parts that go with the trailer. Another guy would be in there doing some spot welding on the metal on the trailers to get them ready for the next day. And a cleanup guy. And another guy making dies for the stamping plant."

ONE OF DALE'S friend's on the line was Henry Kelly. Henry's entrance into Willow Grove was not due in part to family as was Dale's. "I went to an unemployment office and they gave me an address to visit to see if I'd like going to work there because I told them I'd do anything," Henry recalled. "It happened to be a place that was owned by U-Haul at the time, called Willow Grove Manufacturing Company. Fairly close to my home. My father drove me over there. He was outside in the car when I went in for the interview. I talked to a gentleman who was the plant manager at the time; his name was Ed Volts. I filled out a small paper application. And Ed looked at it, and he said, 'Most of your schooling was in a parochial school,' he said, 'Why aren't you going to look for a job in another area? Why are you going to work in a manufacturing plant when most of your subjects were geared toward commercial business?' And I said, 'Well, to be truthful with you, my dad's out in the car and he told me either I go get a job today or he's going to take me to the draft board.' And Ed laughed a little bit, and he said, 'Okay kid, we don't want to put you in the service yet so why don't you come back in tomorrow morning at seven o'clock?'"

Kelly went to work carrying sheet metal to be stamped. He was a solid worker and paid strict attention to direction, almost too strict. "The manager had told me that Eli was going to be my boss," remembered Kelly. "'You do what Eli asks you to do. It doesn't matter. We got a lot of people working here doing various jobs, and Eli is the guy who's going to give you instructions.' That stuck in my mind, and I happened to be getting something for Eli, and I walked past this one area in the operation where there were two gentlemen working in the corner. It appeared like they were working by themselves. One fella, who I later found out was L.S. Shoen, was putting parts into a fixture. And the other fella had a hood on, and was a tall gentleman, and that turned out to be Hap Carty. They were actually working on a prototype for a new trailer. L.S. called me over and asked me to get something for him. And I told him I work for a gentleman by the name of Eli and he's the only one who's supposed to give me instructions . . . and I think I walked away from them. Then I heard him and the other guy laughing as I walked away. Later on in the day I found out who they were, and I don't mind telling you, I was pretty embarrassed."

SAM WAS STILL not into the suit-and-tie rigmarole of corporate life. He loved the factory, and developing new products and manufacturing techniques. It was a quality that endeared him to the factory workers. "If I had seen Sam out in the street," said John Zuransky, "I would've given him a few dollars so maybe he could get some new clothes. I mean, he was a down-to-earth person, nothing fancy about him. You'd think he was just an average working person."

Sam's down-to-earth demeanor and appreciation for people working in manufacturing probably helped keep U-Haul plant workers from unionizing. It's remarkable that through this time and until the present day, the manufacturing plants of U-Haul are nonunion. "Some of the plants had union problems," remembered Jerry Ayres. "I know the one we had in Chicago, it started getting big union problems. But the area where the shop was at or where the plant was at sort of degraded anyway, went into more of a slum. Periodically the unions would come in. One time they had a vote but they got voted down so bad they gave up on it for quite a few years. They tried it again, got voted down—no one was interested."

One attempt to unionize brought Vin Kiley head to head with an infamous union boss. "I was in Michigan," Kiley recounted, "and I knew Pops Fouts, who ran the plant, very well, and I knew Fats Sheldon, the fellow that ran the marketing company. We're sitting there eating breakfast and Pops said, 'You know,' I said, 'Pops, I don't know, but I better know what's going on. Something's wrong here.' Well, it seems Fats Sheldon, who ran the rental company was going to organize it [into a union], and was going to go into Jimmy Hoffa's local. What the hell do you do? So I got on the phone and called Hap. He's having a crisis out in Willow Grove; Ed Volts has been let go, the shit hit the fan out there. Hap said, 'You got to handle it yourself, Vin.' So I said to Fouts, 'Do you have a motel that can get us in a corner off by ourselves?' We got two rooms adjoining. So, anyhow, I bought some beer and some bourbon, and got all the field managers that came to town over to the motel. I got them pretty well bombed. I tore the phone out of the wall in their room, kept the one in my room. They never did make the meeting, and we never did see Mr. Hoffa. Hap finally got in about eight that night. They had to stay anyhow. They were in no shape to go anywhere. Anyhow, I was dead tired, that's exhausting, plus I was scared. I mean I knew who Mr. Hoffa was. Anyway, we went to sleep, but before we went, I piled all the beer cans on top of each other against the door. It must have been six in the morning, maybe five. Bill had been in the other room, and he bangs on the door, and the cans fall. I headed for the window."

Unions weren't needed in the U-Haul System, it was that simple. Health insurance was covered, wages were sufficient and System members could participate in the Fleet Owner Program.

With the success of Willow Grove, other manufacturing plants opened up or were acquired by U-Haul. "We had purchased a facility up in Akron [Ohio]," said Henry Kelly. "The name of the facility was Steiner Body. What they did at this facility was make the giant tire trucks."

"When they took [Steiner Body] over, they were manufacturing trucks with lifts on the back of them for Firestone," remembered Bill Carpenter. "Firestone would go out and service construction businesses with tires, and they'd have that lift back there to lift the tires. And they were still manufacturing them at that time. It was in the contract when [Sam] bought the building."

"But we had purchased it to build trailers," recalled Henry Kelly. "And at this time, of course, this is still probably in '58, we had no motor vehicles, we were strictly trailers. Ed Volts [prior to being let go from Willow Grove] called a bunch of us single guys into a room one day, and he said, 'We bought a new facility up in Akron, Ohio, and we need people to go up and help start an assembly line.' It was four of us that volunteered. There was a fella who did painting, named Dale Green. He was one of the four. Only one had a car out of this group. And we all jumped in his car. Packed up what little belongings we had, which all probably fit into one little box. And we went out to Akron. We still built the giant tire trucks there. I guess it was a lucrative business. And we put a trailer assembly plant down through one part of the building."

While Kelly and the other three men from Willow Grove taught the workers at Steiner Body how to make trailers, he received an education of his own: "They took this kid from Philadelphia under their wing and taught me how to build truck bodies. They built their own handles. They built their own cabinets. I developed quite a bit of a trade or a craft doing that."

It proved to be a smart apprenticeship choice for Kelly: "I think it was approximately toward the end of '58 to the beginning of '59, I got a call from this gentleman Bill Jakubek, who was somewhat running manufacturing at the time. He asked me if I could go down into Akron. [Kelly had been in Hammond, Indiana assisting with the plant there.] They were going to send a truck body from a company in Pennsylvania called Banner—it was a kit—and would I help put this kit together and put it on a chassis, and it was a Dodge chassis."

AS 1959 ROARED ahead, two more innovations helped U-Haul catch up to and quash the competition.

The first was an issue that beleaguered designers, like Safford, for years: tandem trailers. A December 1956 *U-Haul News* illustrates the perils of tandem trailers. There are two photos of a trailer and a car, both wrecked. The caption below the car reads, "Anyone who doesn't believe in taking extra care while towing a trailer [*especially a large tandem*] should take another look at this one of a competitor's after a fatal collision with the station wagon."

People rented tandems because they provided a bigger payload. While trailers allowed people to move their possessions, larger households could not be packed into UVs or FVs. At this point in American history, family homes were growing, acquiring televisions, larger refrigerators, and washers and dryers. *Fortune* magazine observed, "Never has a whole people spent so much money on so many expensive things in such an easy way as Americans are today."

U-Haul lost customers to the competition because it lacked a tandem trailer. U-Haul did campaign strongly against tandems as safety hazards, but resisted the urge to just churn one out to appease an expectant customer base unless it was safe and not prone to swaying and rollovers. Still, the public U-Haul served made it clear: they needed a trailer with a larger payload.

"In 1957, we added four-wheel tandem trailers," said Logan Frank. "We had none. The competition had them and they had what we called the 'suicide undercarriages.' In other words, there were four hanger bars, and if you ran one of the tandems off the road it would sway and come back on the road, and sway to the side, and just keep swaying. So we came up with what we called a Fayette undercarriage, which between the tires had one hanger, no hanger, and a hanger at the front. So when it went off the road, the tires on one side would never come together. No matter what, they would stay the same distance apart, and so we considered that safe. At that time, we quit criticizing tandems and began praising tandems because we had a good one, a safe one."

In a September 1960 *U-Haul News,* there is an article about Logan Frank's new marketing strategy for the U-Haul tandems based on his own experience with that kind of trailer. Logan called it "Look Underneath," a riff on another program U-Haul had: the Look Inside Program. The program was intended to show off a trailer's cleanliness and quality craftsmanship. The article explained Logan's efforts to get people to look underneath the trailers. "When Logan Frank, the U-Haul Company Manager [*sic*] in Florida heard that the U-Haul Tandem [*sic*] trailers were far safer than all of the competitors' tandems, he wanted to find out for himself if this was true," the article reads. "So he rented a few of the competitors' tandems and took them out on trial runs to see how they towed. He found out fast. He nearly got himself killed when the tandem he was pulling went into a violent whipping action. This made him a believer and now he is working hard to educate the public that U-Haul has the safest equipment. In addition to the 'look inside' program actively being promoted in the Florida area, now the pitch is 'look underneath.'"

Was it true? Could a tandem carry a significant payload? A publicity photo for the new tandems appeared in the March 1960 *U-Haul News* showing just how much could be loaded in a tandem: beds, a stove, a crib, dressers, a washer and dryer and other household items. The tandem offered customers more payload space without sacrificing the safety of their family or household goods.

* * *

THE PREEMINENT U-HAUL innovation, which stuck a dagger into the heart of the competition, came in 1959: full-size trucks. Widespread rentals, however, were not available until 1960. Prior to 1959, only professional moving companies had them. Now, trucks would be available to the general public. The fear it must have struck in the competition was something akin to the introduction of tanks in World War I. It defied convention and imagination. Until then, the rental business dealt in trailers. Nationwide and National could not upgrade their trailers. U-Haul had, and they had given them a makeover. Now they brought in trucks, which could be rented at a reasonable price, and the competition cringed. Dick Wrublik, whose idea it was to get into truck rentals, said the move gave U-Haul "a competitive advantage."

It certainly gave the psychological edge to U-Haul System members. 1959 is often cited as a banner year among them. "It changed our whole concept," said Ron Frank, "from just a few trailers to 'Hey this thing is going to go,' because people like those trucks. Customers just love those things. So I can see that as a milestone."

"I know the year I felt good was when we came out with the trucks, that'd be '59," said Vin Kiley. "I felt like, 'Boy, we are going to do it, we are going to do it.' People kept saying, 'I wish you had a truck, I wish you had a truck. The trailer was a little too small. Do you know where I can get a truck?' Then we started coming out with them. It was, I felt, big."

"We realized that we were not only in the trailer-rental business, but we were in transportation," said Henry Kelly. "There was a certain amount of people who were going to move around the country. We're getting to where we're many years after World War II, and people are starting to gain possessions. And a little bit more possessions than [would fit] in a trailer. With them gaining more possessions, they needed something bigger to move with. We realized the only way to do this was to get into trucks."

The introduction of trucks was welcomed by the American public. As historian Alan Brinkley noted, "Prosperity fueled such longtime consumer crazes as the automobile. Consumers also responded eagerly to the development of such new products as dishwashers, garbage disposals, television and high-fidelity and stereo records."

Symbolically, trucks sounded the death knell for the competition. Practically, though, the first trucks were really only symbols. "The first trucks we had were Dodge—flathead, six-cylinder Dodges," said Logan Frank. "They would barely pull up a hill empty. And if you put anything in them, they wouldn't get up the hill."

There was a buzz throughout the ARCOA office. "Everyone was excited," said Jacque Hedwall, "and so anxious to see what the public was going to think of all this."

U-Haul entered the truck business cautiously. "We started by buying three trucks, all used," remembered Jim Shaw. "We bought them in California. One had been a Hertz truck on a local rental in the Midwest, and some guy had bought it when it was used, and moved his goods west. Up in Portland, they bought a little company that had somewhere in the neighborhood of thirty or forty trucks, but some of them didn't run. So that was the start, all strictly on the West Coast, and they were all used trucks. It was just kind of an entry into trucks, and basically we used them for locals. We tried to encourage one-ways, but we didn't know how to do it. Then in '59, we took delivery of the first new trucks. At that stage, I knew Dick Wrublik was a key person behind trucks, making some key decisions about equipment."

"How did I get in the truck-rental business?" asked Dick Wrublik. "I know how I did it. But I don't know of anybody telling me to do it." Wrublik went down to California to meet with a dealer, who, according to Wrublik was a forty-year veteran of rentals. "I was talking to him about buying the trailers, you know, and he wanted to give me the trucks." He visited this man at least once a month to assess the feasibility of trucks.

Wrublik's first concern was insurance. "He told me everything about insurance, repair, everything. And it was exactly the way he told it. Insurance was nothing if he didn't rent many to the truckers. We only had trouble with the truckers." What Wrublik discovered was that people were timid about getting behind the wheel of a large truck. They had never been there before. This caused them to be more cautious while driving, more so than when they were driving a car. Naturally, the potential for accidents seemed less likely because nontruckers were hypervigilant. Truckers, on the other hand, were supremely confident and that attitude at times could cause them to let their guard down and be less observant on the road.

The other source of potential concern was the support network, but U-Haul already had a system designed to support trailers. And as Wrublik found out, "It didn't cost us hardly anything extra to support the trucks, as far as fieldmen. They went to visit dealers. They had trucks and trailers. They still only went to the one place. And a lot of the work they do is the same whether it's trucks or trailers: check the contracts, et cetera. In other words, in a sense, we were developing a second, equal cash system and we had no overhead to account for it."

An added bonus came in an unforeseen clientele. "For a smaller business that had shipments coming in, instead of making so many trips with something maybe smaller like a little Econoline or one of those van things, now they could rent a truck," said Jacque Hedwall explaining how companies like UPS would use U-Haul trucks during Christmas to handle the larger volume of deliveries.

IT IS AMAZING, and a testament to Sam's choice of people to work at ARCOA, that in the years following Anna Mary's death, while Sam dealt with his grief, U-Haul continued to grow. The company did not just maintain the status quo. O'Donnell, Safford, Carty and all the rest did not keep U-Haul running until Sam's return; they expanded it. This is a prime example of why U-Haul succeeded over its competitors—it wasn't hamstrung by centralized authority, with one person calling the shots, or a large confederation constantly bickering with one another. Instead, U-Haul thrived thanks to a network of people, buoyed by the System, supporting one another. AFMs supported dealers, who supported customers. Rental company managers supported the AFMs, and ARCOA provided support for the rental companies, a theme Sam drove home later in 1962.

Ironically, the first truck rental, like the first trailer one-way rental, was the recipient of some bad luck, which was good. "The story way back when on this thing [U-Haul] was, if the first rental on anything went bad, it was an omen that things were going to work out," explained Jerry Ayres. "First local rental, they lost a trailer. Then when they had the first one-way from Portland down to San Francisco, that trailer never showed up again. Then when they got into trucks, the first one built, one of the boys went out there and was going to drive it back from Ohio, and not realizing it had a big canopy over the top, took out the first gas station canopy. Totally wrecked that truck up. And the trucks came out very good, obviously. So it was kind of an omen if you try something and the first one failed then it was going to be a success."

THESE INNOVATIONS CRIPPLED the competition like Henry Bohannon in Florida. Logan Frank was well acquainted with Bohannon. They were friends as well as rivals. "The two presidents of Nationwide and National were in Florida," said Logan. "I was twenty-four years old. So I was young and these guys [Nationwide and National] were old-timers. They were, as I said, the big dogs on the block. In Orlando, they were the Hamilton Brothers and they wouldn't even talk to me. I tried to get into their office. The president of National Trailer rentals, H.D. Bohannon, was in Tampa. Mr. Bohannon was a strong, independent, big guy, but I dropped by four or five times and finally one day we went and had an iced tea together, and one thing led to another, and in late 1959, I opened Mr. Bohannon as a U-Haul dealer. And we converted the National sign from 'National Trailer Rentals' to 'U-Haul Trailer Rentals.'" Eventually, Ron Frank converted George Nelson's Nationwide dealership to a U-Haul dealership. And one of the largest markets for rentals was securely in the hands of U-Haul.

A story about Henry D. Bohannon, president of National Trailer rentals, in a June 1960 *U-Haul News* was titled, "Welcome to U-Haul, Henry." A major triumph, yes, but the article is not boastful, considering the importance of this event. The article mentions that Bohannon was a founder of National Trailer Rental. The article lauds Bohannon for having "one of the System's finest examples of effective trailer display." Above his picture, the caption reads, "We are proud to have high-caliber rental operators like Bohannon in the U-Haul System." There was no crowing, or gloating; it was a demonstration of quiet class.

L. S. Shoen in the ARCOA computer room, 1962.

The U-Haul Primary Service Objective, from the 1962 Lecture Tour.

Tom Safford presenting at the 1962 Lecture Tour.

A U-Haul trailer in use, 1961.

Prairie, Texas, 1962. Jim Oakley placed a tandem at his office in Grand Prairie on MacArthur Blvd. Logan Frank mounted the first U-Haul trailer on a pole in 1956, in Orlando, Florida.

The first modular sign used by the U-Haul Company, 1964.

Logan and Dee Frank at the Tampa (Florida) State Fair, with a U-Haul table display, 1960.

Trix U-Haul trailer display in grocery store, 1962.

A dealer stands in a sea of trailers in Oklahoma City, 1962.

Jim and Sophia Shoen stand with one of their father's trailers, 1963.

A Beetle Bailey cartoon ad, 1963.

L. S. Shoen, 1961.

L. S. Shoen at his desk, 1962.

A U-Haul service truck and trailers, 1963

U-Haul Service station dealer and his servicemen.

The C-1 bumper hitch, 1964. The same basic hitch is still in use today.

Jack Lorentz

Pat Crahan in front of new marketing company office in Oklahoma, 1964.

U-Haul dealer Mike Morelli, 1978.

Dick Wrublick, Vin Kiley and Tom O'Donnell, 1963.

Jim Shaw

Harry DeShong Sr.

Willow Grove Manufacturing truck fleet, 1961.

U-Haul pressman at Willow Grove Manufacturing, 1961.

The production team at Warrington Manufacturing, 1964.

Shining up a new "U" trailer at Steiner Body in Akron, Ohio, 1961.

10

TO BE RECKONED WITH

THE COMPETITION WAS feeling the hurt by 1960. In a now-famous moment in U-Haul history (a favorite anecdote of Hap Carty's), Jim Simer showed Nationwide exactly what it was up against. Simer, in a gravelly voice reminiscent of Clint Eastwood, tells the story that while at a restaurant in Prineville, Oregon, Simer overheard a representative from Nationwide trailers. "The guy was running our U-Haul System down," said Simer, "telling some other people our trailers are no good, and it made me mad and I invited him outside. I called him a liar. They called the police, and [I] told the police how the guy took the first swing and I decked him. Anyway, I made a believer out of him."

Fighting was not common for staving off competition, but the story stands as a reminder that the men working in the field had an overwhelming feeling of pride in their work. U-Haul was the standard in trailer rentals and the only company renting trucks as 1960 began.

The network of dealers had swelled and U-Haul needed quality fieldmen for these positions. Simer was like many other fieldmen. There were three hundred AFMs at this time. Many of the U-Haul hires were World War II veterans, who in the years following the war took on factory jobs or other blue-collar jobs. In Simer's case, he had been a boilermaker at a shipyard. But there was a growing restlessness among returning soldiers. They had been shipped overseas, and had seen Europe or the Pacific, and coming home to put down roots was unenviable. The job of a fieldman beckoned to people like Jim Simer and Bill Carpenter. Their pride was a type molded on the battlefields in the Pacific and Europe, which brought forth a fighting spirit. They refused to back down an inch, and knew how to move in only one direction: forward. "The truth was the country was changing at a remarkable rate," writes David Halberstam, "and a generation would soon come to power whose confidence and ambition had been intensified by both World War II and the dynamism of the postwar economy."

U-Haul hired many veterans from this battle-tested generation. Their battlefield experience in World War II meshed well with the tough work ethic required of fieldmen, and these were key to helping U-Haul succeed. Many fieldmen had seen combat and lived in foxholes for most of the war. Kermit Shoen fought in the Pacific, and earned a Silver Star, one of the nation's highest military awards for gallantry. He was even awarded the patch of the vaunted Marine 1st Division. Simer, too, served in the Pacific, for which he was awarded the Bronze Star. He was a point man for his platoon, an assignment that generally brought with it a short life expectancy or the long-lasting memories that unspeakable war begets. Bill Carpenter, another new AFM in 1960, fought in Europe in many major battles, including the Battle of the Bulge. He was one of the first American soldiers to witness the aftermath of the Malmédy massacre, at which eighty-four unarmed American soldiers were killed by the Germans. Vern Olson, a rental company president on the West Coast, had volunteered for service as a seventeen-year-old. He went on to command tanks in Europe.

Veterans' determination and resolve were stronger than that of many other people. It helped to make them men to be reckoned with. For Vern Olson, who survived the destruction of three of his tanks, a service rig easily provided more comfort and safety than his tanks did. Jim Simer perhaps put it best. "After living in a fox-hole, living in the field rig felt like the Hilton," he said.

Little procedural details mattered to them, a carryover from military life. Simer, for instance, always checked the books first when he arrived at the dealer, "You'd get out there, and you're working and you'd get all dirty and so I wanted to be clean to do the books. Then I'd go out and put on my coveralls and do the repair." It was not policy, only personal preference.

THE JOB HAD changed little since the early days. The area covered was smaller in some cases. There were no cross-country runs for fieldmen. While the area was more limited, the number of dealers was higher. (By this point, U-Haul had expanded into Canada, too.) Fieldmen were now on the road longer because they were servic-ing many more dealers, not covering large tracts of land. The increase in dealers had also led to dealer classifications resembling the minor league baseball structure: AAA, AA, A. These classifica-tions had names: AAA dealers were "Key Dealers"; AA dealers were "Specialty Dealers"; and A dealers were "Standard Dealers."

The classification system was based on nine factors, all related to dealer performance: Sales proficiency, promotion proficiency, lot facilities, cooperation with other dealers in sharing equipment, equipment control, keeping a firm grip over traffic control or violations or evasions (a nod to the Traffic Department's work), reporting practices, care of equipment and gross rental volume. The last factor was established for AAA and AA dealers, and listed earn-ings for May and November that had to be met according to the population of the town the dealer was in. A Key Dealer (AAA) in a city of 100,000 had to gross $80 in the month of May, the start of the rental season.

The classification system arose because the increased amount of products U-Haul rented meant that the best dealers possible were needed to market and maintain them. The new product list included hand trucks, tow bars, car-top carriers and furniture pads. Some of the products, such as trucks and larger tandem trailers, were quite expensive. Only AAA dealers could rent trucks, and those trucks had to be returned to another AAA dealer. This was done in part because AAA dealers had the facilities to handle simple truck maintenance such as changing the oil and oil filter.

"Field reps couldn't repair trucks very well," explained Phil Schnee. "I'm not a mechanic. I can repair a trailer—I can rebuild a trailer. But when it came to trucks I wasn't a mechanic. I couldn't sit there and analyze a motor. If the oil is dirty or the fluid levels were low, or something like that, I knew how to check that. But mechanically, no, so we had to have someone to do that. So we had the shops, you know the dealerships."

Once a dealer was eligible for any classification, he had to post a $100 bond for every level of classification he rose to, which was quite a departure from the early years when dealers simply agreed to rent U-Haul trailers. The bonds served a dual purpose. The bonds were invested in dealer fleets. Therefore, an AAA dealer posted $300 in bonds, which were invested in three different dealer fleets. At this point, U-Haul had no problem finding dealers, and this system of bonds encouraged dealer responsibility by rewarding it. The potential forfeiture of bonds discouraged dealer dishonesty. It also provided U-Haul with extra revenue to build more trailers.

The potential loss of bonds and revenue from a fleet would seem enough of a deterrent for dealers to avoid dishonesty, but some still tried to take advantage of the System. One-way rentals were hard to scam because the contracts were numbered, and if a contract was missing from the dealer's book, but nowhere to be found among the copies of the one-way rental contracts, it was likely the dealer had not written the contract or had thrown it away and pocketed the customer's money. But there was always another dealer on the other end of the one-way rental who ensured accurate account auditing. Local rentals were a little easier to cheat on since the product was returned to the dealership of origin and if a dealer simply did not report it, there was no smoking gun, such as a truck arriving at another dealership with no record of such a one-way rental on file with ARCOA.

"Sometimes these dealerships would use our money," said Phil Schnee. "They had the money there that they did business with. They had our money that they were supposed to report on Monday morning. They would hold back contracts. They would keep the money and do something else with it. I had one dealer who bought a wrecker, you know a tow truck, with U-Haul Company's money. When I came in to service him as a field rep, I was noticing the contracts were dated six months back. He was reporting contracts from six months ago, so what happened to those other [current] ones? And we got to doing an audit on him, and we found out the guy owes about twenty thousand dollars. There was a new wrecker out there. You knew damn well where that came from. We had some problems."

Jim Simer had zero tolerance for dealer fraud. He shut down one dealer early on in his tenure with U-Haul. "L.S. opened him up and [the dealer] said I couldn't close him because I couldn't find another dealer." Simer admitted it was intimidating. "I thought I'd hear about it," he said. "This guy told me later L.S. said, 'He's the fieldman in that area. He's running it. There's nothing I can do.' That's one thing I liked about [U-Haul]. I couldn't believe they put you in charge of an area and they meant it. You were in charge of it . . . that's all there was to it."

His next step was finding a new dealer. He took the trucks and opened Shorty Shepard as the new AAA dealer in Pendleton, Oregon. "Best dealer that ever was. Better location, more display, and he wound up doing ten times the business the first guy was doing," said Simer.

Shorty and his wife were later featured in *U-Haul News,* according to Simer, because of their house. "They call it their U-Haul house," Simer said. "Their commissions paid for this house, and it was a nice house. They even had a room for me when I came into town. They called it my room."

Another hazard AFMs still faced was bodily harm when doing recoveries. Every AFM has a recovery story. Bill Carpenter raided a remote part of Kentucky with the local sheriff to recover a trailer that was in bad shape. When a previous U-Haul System member had gone to make the recovery, the person living there had brandished a gun. For Carpenter, though, the recovery was probably nothing compared to his days in Europe during World War II, and although dangerous, it was still less stressful than the days when he ran a gasoline station.

BILL CARPENTER IS another interesting member of the System. During his U-Haul career, he was a dealer, an AFM and a rental company manager. Ironically, his entry into U-Haul came about because a Nationwide dealer in his town had closed. That dealership had been operated by a friend with whom Carpenter was hesitant to compete. He did not want to step on anyone's toes. Once Nationwide closed, however, Carpenter pursued a U-Haul dealership. "In the Gasoline Dealers' Association magazine, there was an ad that said if you wanted to be a [U-Haul] dealer, send it in," recalled Carpenter. Of course the traffic to Elkins, West Virginia, was not anywhere near the level at which Ralph Shivers might have classified it as a sump; Carpenter did not get his first trailer for a few months.

Bill Carpenter understood firsthand the stresses a dealer went through in order to make his service station profitable. A service station's revenue was derived from the sale of tires, batteries and accessories (TBA). Gas brought in the least amount of money. The business did, however, prepare him for the work of the fieldman in one way. "Then it [service stations] was all built on service. That's the way you got most of the customers—service," Carpenter explained. Before potential customers would look to a dealer for other services, the extra effort had to be made, "If you didn't clean the windows on a person's car, they didn't want to buy anything from you," remembered Carpenter. Some even insisted that the *inside* of their windows be cleaned as well.

"Dealers like myself," explained Carpenter, "we were making six to seven cents a gallon, and we did all that free work for that. If a man came in, he got the same service if he bought a dollar's worth of gas or ten dollar's worth. Very few of them bought ten dollar's worth because at thirty, thirty-five cents a gallon, they wouldn't haul much more than ten dollar's worth."

Carpenter left the service station behind when a pending gas war, fueled by oil companies and their local representatives, appeared ready to break out in Elkins. "Everybody started cutting prices on the gasoline," said Carpenter. "I didn't want to sell it that way. You're only making six to seven cents a gallon; no sense cutting it down to make it one or two. I didn't want to have to pay to have somebody out there at the pumps all the time pumping gasoline and making a penny or two pennies a gallon." So he decided to make a career switch and became an AFM for U-Haul.

THE GAS WARS the oil companies had spawned forced Carpenter out of the service station business. When he entered the U-Haul System, he faced still more problems with the oil companies. Many of their representatives detested the U-Haul trailers on the lots of their service stations. "When I was a fieldman, Shell didn't want [U-Haul trailers] in the District," said Carpenter. Simer, too, often had to battle oil reps, who would move U-Haul displays (or the trailers themselves) off the lot.

"Oil reps were always negative toward U-Haul because they thought we were doing business out of their property without any expense on our part," said Dale Green. "And I think we were worthwhile for the service stations owners: give them some extra income to stay in business. And some of the oil company reps did realize that and others didn't, so they weren't all bad."

Such antagonism put the service station owner, who was an independent businessman, in the middle of two companies fighting over control of *his lot*. In order to soothe mounting tensions, many U-Haul AFMs worked in a proactive manner to get to know and work with oil company reps who worked in their respective areas.

Logan Frank had an issue of his own with an oil rep in St. Petersburg, Florida. "I was there talking to the dealer and he wasn't keeping the display right," said Logan. "See, if you let the dealers have an overload of trailers, and the display is sloppy, everything else [in the station] is too. Well of course the oil company would gripe at you. If I was an oil company rep, I would have screamed bloody murder at some U-Haul dealer because they were overloaded; the display was not straight and so forth. So sometimes we were our own worst enemy. Anyway, I remember this one case. I was in talking to the dealer, and [the oil rep] drove up in a white Ford. I saw him coming, so I went out of the station to his car. I introduced myself, 'I'm Logan with U-Haul.' He immediately started frowning. I said to him, 'I'd like your help today with [the dealer] to make sure that these trailers are straight. Because if they're not straight, I may have to pull them out.' And it took him aback, you know, because he was coming there to tell me to get them out. After about an hour or two of talking to him—we had a Coke together— finally he got friendly and we left the trailers there. I think he saw we were regular people and were not parasites."

"And we had an interest in keeping everything looking good," interjected Dee Frank.

"In that case, we had helped clean up the dealer's lube bay," continued Logan. "We helped him for about an hour, so we could put a small sign up in there. It kind of took [the oil rep] off guard." Logan had no qualms cleaning service station restrooms either. The message he wanted the oil reps to know was clear: U-Haul does not just drop off its trailers. U-Haul had an interest in the dealer's success as much as the oil reps did.

Bill Carpenter, like Logan, made a potential adversary his friend. "I got to know the representative and got to be good friends with him, and I finally ended up with several Shell dealerships in DC."

Jim Simer invited oil reps to his dealer meetings, and found that simple entertainment relieved hostilities. "We had these little movies called *Sandy McTavish*," he said. "It was a little cartoon about renting trailers and never letting a customer get away, and I'd show that. And, even the oil reps thought that was the greatest little advertisement [U-Haul] had." U-Haul was committed to the customer, and the representatives from the oil companies saw that. U-Haul was not simply taking up unused space on service station lots, it provided an additional source of income for station owners and another service they might offer to their customers.

COOPERATION AMONG DEALERS received greater emphasis as it was necessary to a dealer's success. Some dealers, however, viewed cooperation as lost revenue. An article in *U-Haul News* at this time encouraged dealers to "[g]et acquainted with your neighboring dealers," because, "[i]f you have a customer who insists on renting a trailer not in your stock, and substitution won't work, don't turn him away. If there is such a model in the area on any other dealer's lot, you are entitled to it." The same courtesy and privilege was supposed to be extended to other dealers in need as well. The article goes on to say, "Dealers who work hand in hand can keep a surprising amount of rental business within the System . . . business which might otherwise go to competition."

Bill Carpenter tried to facilitate this cooperation by placing dealers close to one another. In one instance, he had three corners of an intersection occupied by U-Haul dealers. "It helped them," Carpenter explained, "because then instead of having five trailers here and five up there, either one of them had ten. You just trade all the way around."

But the dealer–cooperation effort was not always harmonious. As Dee Frank said, "[S]ometimes there was contention between the dealers, 'You've got a trailer; I want it.'"

Two men who were known for resolving disputes over dealer cooperation were Hap Carty and Logan Frank. Their methods of conflict resolution, while contrasting, rubbed off on Henry Kelly. Although Kelly primarily worked in manufacturing, he was still influenced by the two men and their methods of working in the field. "One of the advantages I had with knowing the regional directors such as Hap and Logan, who were our top field generals at the time," Henry recalled, "was the way they did business: what they talked about, how they operated, how they encouraged people in their jobs. I liked the management style of both of them. One was a little stronger, Hap. The other, Logan, more or less wanted to encourage and teach people. Their styles stick with me today, and they were two good mentors for me."

Frank Lyons, Hap's brother-in-law, saw Hap's forcefulness first-hand when dealing with two quarreling dealers. "We had to go down to Falls Church, Virginia," remembered Frank. "We had a dealer down there who ran a service station. Then we also had a dealer right behind the service station who was just a dealer, not a service station. Someone would call their dealership wanting to rent a trailer, and they'd say, 'Yeah, come on down.' [The customer] had to drive right by the gas station to get to this guy's lot. Well, when the guy who ran the gas station saw them coming down, and it looked like they were going to get a trailer, he'd run out and stop them . . . and he'd rent them the trailer. [The customer] didn't know the difference. So finally [the lot owner] got fed up with it and went up to the gas station and tore the phone off the wall and threw it out the door. There were unique situations—this was unique. Obviously it didn't happen all the time. And Hap's way of dealing with it was, 'Look, you guys straighten this out or I'm going to shut you both down.' And they got it straightened out."

Logan's method was a bit softer, but no less potent. His philosophy in dealing with people, he said, was: "Forcefulness does not exclude tactfulness, and tactfulness does not exclude forcefulness." He exhibited this maxim with a Mobil station dealer who gave him the cold shoulder. "He would not even look up at me," said Logan. "He was at his desk. He wouldn't even look at me. This man wouldn't speak to the guy [a U-Haul dealer] who had the Texaco station. So after about the third visit, he saw we were going to work, and we got acquainted with him [the Mobil dealer]. I got him in the truck and we headed toward the Texaco station. He said, 'Where are you going?' 'Well, I'm going to go over here and get Mr. Tossi [the Texaco dealer].' He said, 'Oh, no. Not him.' I said, 'Oh, yeah.' So I went and got him. We went and had iced tea, and before long I had them shaking hands."

Dealer relationships were important and dealer meetings helped sustain them. However, the office etiquette shown to the dealers went a long way as well. "One of the mottos we had in all the offices I had anything to do with," said Dee Frank, "was that if a dealer steps inside the door, they're to be treated like a king." This motto reminded the people in the office that it was the dealer making money for U-Haul. "We wanted them to know that our office was there to help them find their needs and get the solution, so that they would be proud that they were U-Haul dealers. Therefore, if an oil rep got on them about certain things, [the dealers] were behind U-Haul because they knew that they were making money. They knew that we were treating them just like family."

There still was no manual to be a fieldman, but Logan Frank's lecture, "How a Dealer Can and Will Do His Job," was as appropriate in 1962 as it was when he was figuring the job out in 1954. He envisioned an AFM as "one to be reckoned with." To earn this reputation, an AFM had to build dealer cooperation, work with the oil reps and work for the dealers. "An area field manager can only handle so many dealers, but if you are a man or woman to be reckoned with and you got thirty dealers, you can have thirty business friends. You can know them personally and they'll call on you. Those things helped."

The AFM was the first line of contact with the dealers, who dealt directly with the customers. "It was like [the AFMs] were running a small marketing company," explained Dee Frank.

"The success of a group of dealers depends a lot on the area field manager," said Logan. "Now some dealers will do well no matter what because they have to. Old-time dealers, they see these field managers, and they look out the window, 'Look here comes a new one. What do you want?' But if a field manager is to be reckoned with, after two or three visits, [the dealer] will look out the window and say, 'Here comes Bill. Come on in, Bill.' In other words, he'll see that this guy is to be reckoned with. Not that he's a smart aleck or overly forceful, but you know the person's to be reckoned with. [Dealers] can size up a guy fast, and if you're to be reckoned with, they're glad to see you."

11

E X KH = R

AS HAS BEEN mentioned, many U-Haul System members described the company as a big family. Often they use familial descriptions for people in the company. Sam was referred to as "the Old Man." That was part of the company's appeal, its early charm.

Accordingly, the company itself survived its infancy literally because of family. The two founders were a husband and wife, living on her parents' farm. Once they started to need other employees, they looked to family. "That's another way you got started: Relations," said Ralph Shivers. "Hap worked for him 'cause Hap was cheap, and Hap was Anna Mary's brother. Another guy who worked early in the game was Martin Zerbes, he was a relation of Sam's. Kerm Shoen, Ken Shoen, cousins, I guess, went to work for him. I did. My two brothers did. My parents did. That's how this damn thing got going was him snagging on to relations of either his wife or himself." His brother Ramon worked in the shop. Margaret Carty, Anna Mary's younger sister, did office work. As other people came to work for U-Haul, they were welcomed into the family.

Some of these System members brought in their own family as well. Jacque Hedwall came to work because her mom had worked at ARCOA with Ralph Shivers. U-Haul was her first choice. "My mom loved her job," Hedwall noted. "She had already been here about a year, year and a half. She just said, 'It's a nice company and you'd really like it.'"

Ron Green brought in his brother Dale. Similarly, Ron Frank joined U-Haul much the same way Dale Green did, on a visit to his brother: "In the summers of 1956 and 1957, I went to Florida in between high school sessions and worked with my older brother. I drove to Florida just to get away from farms and ranches, just something different to do. And I saw Logan having an enjoyable time. He had had a number of different jobs in his life up to that point. *But* I saw that he was really enjoying that. He was getting to move around. He wasn't going to one spot every day. And I thought, 'Well, that ought to be fun.' So when I got out of school I thought, 'I might as well go there.' It can't be any worse than farming and ranching."

When Logan issued Ron his field rig, he also issued a warning. "I remember the first service rig that I had was a 1956, one-ton, Ford truck," said Ron. "It had a rack across the top and a winch to pull the trailers up and down. I don't remember whether it was the water pump or the radiator that was bad, or a combination, but it leaked water. Of course with no water in the internal combustion engine, if you run it and heat it, you're going to ruin the engine. I remember Logan telling me, 'If the truck stops,' in other words if the engine stops, if you ruin the engine, 'you won't have a truck, and you won't be able to do your job, and then you'll be out of work.'"

"I have a personal policy: Hire a relative; a relative works five percent harder," said Logan. "I wasn't mean to him, but the worst thing I could have done to Ron was to show him a bunch of favor over somebody else. That would hurt him."

BY 1962, EVEN the older Shoen boys, Sammy, Mike, Joe and Mark were being prepared to enter the System. They, like their father would do, took a tour in 1962. Theirs was less formal. It was a trip to Canada, which was a new rental area for U-Haul. They went with Tom Safford and repaired trailers, working sixteen-hour days. As Joe Shoen remembered, "It was the first time I understood how big the company was."

The company was moving from one that was small enough to be personable and familial, to one that was so vast it threatened to become a monster outside of Sam's control. An indicator of the dwindling family atmosphere of the early years was seen in the company picnics. "When [U-Haul] got bigger, you didn't see half the people who were there [in the ARCOA headquarters]. The company got so big you didn't know who most of them were. Or I didn't know who everybody was," said Jerry Ayres about the picnics. The building on Hawthorne, that was so sparsely filled early on, was again bursting at the seams.

SAM HAD A dilemma. Much of what had worked for U-Haul in the past was still relevant to the company, but the means of disseminating information were more difficult. Furthermore, management had to be administered in a way that allowed for resourceful, timely thinking, rather than time-consuming checks up the chain of command. But that was not an invitation to reckless independence, which negated any sense of responsibility to higher-ups.

In the past, these problems were commonly addressed through management bulletins. "If we had a problem," said Hap, "A guy would call Sam, or write him a letter or something, and say, 'I got a problem with this.' Instead of Sam picking up the phone and calling him, he would figure out what the answer was, and he'd write it up and call it a bulletin to send to all of us. You didn't have to solve the same problem fifty different ways in fifty different places. It was a good setup."

But with the company's expansion, too many bulletins were going unread, common in any large company. Logan Frank's 1962 lecture, "How a Dealer Can and Will Do His Job," alludes to the problem: "Do you study a bulletin when you receive it, or do you treat it as a newspaper? Glance over it and maybe think to yourself

. . . 'something else out from Arcoa [*sic*] to take up our time and read.'"

Ron Frank best sums up why these bulletins went unread. "When I started with the company, I would get a bulletin from L.S. and I'd read it," he remembered. "I didn't understand what the man was saying." Ron was most likely an exception to the rule, though, because he sought out other, more experienced businessmen to explain the bulletin to him. He didn't just "glance over it" as many others did.

Within the ARCOA building, new hires did not necessarily work out. "We hired a lot of good people," said Tom O'Donnell, "people who were academically in the top of their classes. Very few of them ever worked out. They'd be going around there thinking they were king of the roost, and the next week they'd be gone. That happened all the time."

COMPOUNDING THE PROBLEMS brought on by rapid expansion was the relevance of the headquarters in Portland. Sam had moved his growing family to Palm Springs, California. O'Donnell ran day-to-day operations at ARCOA, while Sam spent his time traversing the country in his plane.

In the years after Anna Mary's death, Sam immersed himself in a variety of studies. One was flying. Again, this was due in part to expanding the network of dealers and rental companies. He saw that driving was costly both in time, gas and hotels. Flying on commercial airlines was expensive if done repeatedly and therefore impractical. In the long run, Sam could learn to fly, purchase a plane and save money transporting himself. Eventually, he, Hap, Logan Frank and Tom O'Donnell flew their own planes purchased by the company. "Instead of giving us a raise, he'd usually give us a new plane," quipped Logan, laughing. "No, he'd give us raises, too."

Portland, though, was no longer the hub for the management trainees. Gone were the days of bringing in groups of aspiring young men who would listen to Sam teach them about U-Haul and business principles before shipping out to Oakland or other locations across the nation. Instead, the trend was for Sam to hire local people to handle the rental companies. Pat Crahan's hiring is an example of this practice. It was done to combat the one advantage the competition had over U-Haul. The rental company manager then hired AFMs, who in turn opened dealers.

Signs also pointed to a move from Portland (which eventually happened in 1967, when the company relocated to Phoenix, Arizona). Part of the reason Sam wanted to move, according to Tom O'Donnell, was "it was just more prestigious being there [Phoenix]. The fact that U-Haul grew up here—he didn't get the prestige here in Portland." The idea of moving was something Sam kicked around quite a bit at this time. At one point he was set on moving the company to Pennsylvania. Duane Swanson even put his house up for sale and had a buyer lined up before Sam changed his mind, partly because of some coercing from O'Donnell. "[H]e was pushing hot to move Arcoa [sic]," recalled O'Donnell. "I was pushing the other way. I argued with him, I don't know how many times. He looked all over. I remember one time, he had me down there with him in Tennessee."

The company, was by no means unorganized, but it was having a personality crisis stemming from a variety of causes: a potential move, the expanding system, new rental products, etc. But one acquisition in particular literally divided the company.

IN 1959, U-HAUL assumed management of Kar-Go, a nationwide chain of trailer rental dealerships. Kar-Go had a sizable inventory of product and a decent dealer network. According to *Management Bulletin No. 165*, the transaction "involved approximately 5,000 trailers and 400 dealers." The conversion would utilize the U-Haul System of dealers, marketing companies and fieldmen already in place.

Kar-Go was supposed to be an alternative to U-Haul rentals: The prices would be lower, but the equipment and protection were comparable to U-Haul. "We would open a dealer with U-Haul or we would open them with Kar-Go," said Logan Frank, "and if [customers] came in to U-Haul and said, 'We'll just go down to

Kar-Go and rent. You're a little high.'We'd say, 'Well, all right, you go there. They're a good bunch down there.'"

Sam believed the Kar-Go Program would be to U-Haul what Ford cars were to Lincolns. When Ralph Shivers heard that analogy, he laughed, and responded, "More like Ford and Edsel."

In a way, the *U-Haul News* of November 19, 1959, announcing U-Haul Company's purchase of the blue trailers, foretold the eventual problems U-Haul would encounter with the Kar-Go takeover. Covered van models accounted for less than ten percent of Kar-Go's fleet. Kar-Go would not supersede U-Haul either: "U-Haul dealers can be assured that their dealership will continue to be of top value and that Arcoa, Inc. [*sic*] and the rental companies fully intend to provide them with more and more services and features." However Kar-Go trailers were of lesser quality, had not been properly repaired and soon became an albatross around the neck of U-Haul.

"They weren't good equipment," said Bill Carpenter. "A lot of them had flat tires; others had automobile tires on them, just not much of a trailer. And they had never had any roadside service. That's what got them in such bad shape. Some of them, you couldn't even walk in the trailer; the floorboards were just rotting out."

The program needed full attention, which it received in 1960. "Went full speed ahead on Kar-go [*sic*]," the bulletin reads. By December 1960, the mood had changed: "Seriously evaluated the Kar-Go System and decided to continue and to convert some U-Haul vans to Kar-Go vans." By 1961, the bulletin concedes, "Kar-go [*sic*] operation failed to show any real potential despite substantial expense and effort. Began program of combining U-Haul and Kar-Go dealers into single type and intermixing trailers."

"Down in Kentucky, there used to be Kar-Go trailers down there . . . You couldn't count them all," remembered Bill Carpenter. "They were just shoved back in the lot if the dealer had an empty lot. They never rented them very much." And from there, Kar-Go faded into oblivion.

* * *

AS YOUNG ENTREPRENEURS, Sam and Bert Layman enjoyed listening to Julian McFadden because they learned how to run their barbershops from an experienced businessman. Sam carried this method of learning over to U-Haul. Sam loved to lecture. This trait could spell disaster for a horribly boring person, but Sam pulled it off with aplomb. Pat Crahan appreciated the impromptu lectures. "I was new, so they arranged that I share a room with Sam," he said, remembering an early road trip he was on. "Back then, and even now, when you travel, you team up. So I was thrown into the briar patch: I had to room with Sam. So I thought, 'Fantastic,' because I had always enjoyed being with him. About Sam: He never carried on a conversation; he always lectured. It was just constant lecture, all the time. And I loved it because I wanted to learn U-Haul. I wanted to know more about it. I liked his lectures. If you mentioned anything, he would lecture on that subject, on and on." Learning was never complete for him or System members. A true student never stops learning. Sam had always been a voracious reader, and he spent considerable time reading about business.

In the '50s Sam held Saturday meetings with his executives that served as tutorials. "Sam was real keen on management principles and getting people educated," Tom O'Donnell said in a 1988 interview. "He got a hold of a book on management that was written by a guy named Davis [*The Fundamentals of Top Management* by Ralph Currier Davis]. And so that was our Bible for a long time. We studied Davis. Each week we'd have a management meeting there at ARCOA, and we would discuss various principles of management from the book."

Sam's lessons did not end at the office. Joe Shoen remembered that around 1961 his father sat the older boys down and gave them a few lessons on management. Perhaps, at some point, Joe saw the equation $E \times KH = R$, a major feature of Sam's magnum opus, his grand work: the 1962 Lecture. Those lessons on the blackboard were Sam's tune-up for his national speaking tour to members of the U-Haul System.

* * *

THE FACTS AND events leading up to the '62 Lecture would seem to indicate that some of the major changes that took place at U-Haul after Anna Mary's passing in 1957 and Sam's subsequent leave of absence might have motivated Sam to rein in the company's upper management. It was, in fact, the opposite. One of his quotes from the lecture, which is not attributed to any particular writer or speaker noted, "Great men seem to use men of great boldness; in reality they are more obedient than others." It could therefore be argued that the purpose of the lecture was motivated partly by the commendable initiative of Tom O'Donnell, Dick Wrublik, Ralph Shivers and Hap Carty, while Sam was away. Their ability to improvise and take purposeful risks was proof that all the management meetings had been useful, and groups of management trainees had learned valuable lessons on delegation and responsibility to the organization as a whole.

Sam had to acquaint new System members as to what had worked for the company in years past. His solution was the same one he used when he came upon a challenge: he went back to the basics. If he could not bring management trainees into ARCOA, he would bring the management training to the new managers and fieldmen. By 1962, what Sam needed was more than a bulletin, but a more concise lecture intended to reach a Systemwide audience.

The lecture tour began on February 5 and continued on through six cities: Willow Grove, Pennsylvania; Atlanta; Chicago; Dallas; Los Angeles; and Portland, Oregon. Sam wasn't the only one who lectured over the two weeks. Hap Carty talked about the responsibilities of the line executive. Tom Safford spoke about staff executives' responsibilities, and designed many of the graphics for the speakers. Jim Oakley, regional director of the Mid-South District, spoke about coordinating the efforts between line and executive staff. Logan Frank, now the South East Regional Director, gave his aforementioned lecture, "How a Dealer Can and Will Do His Job." Their tour was unofficially titled, "Out of the Bars and into the Books." Two-hundred and sixty-five System members attended. Away from the lectures they were introduced to a new idea Sam had to evaluate System members: six tests assessing a person's adaptability and intelligence. Throughout his lecture, these were probably the two most important qualities Sam encouraged System members to embrace.

Sam's portion of the lecture lived far beyond 1962. It is a testament to how well it stuck with his audience, and how well it was applied after the lecture by those who were there. Hap remembered his father, William E. Carty, saying, "It was a Harvard education in thirty pages."

Bill Carpenter, one of the newer System members, saw the opening lecture at Willow Grove. "It was really a good lecture, and he presented it well," he said. "I still have my copy."

"It was a brilliant thing," said Duane Swanson. "He was talking about what marketing was all about and what management was all about, and the difference between a line executive and a staff executive. He came out with all kinds of slogans." The major slogans, or concepts, that came from Sam's lecture and remain with U-Haul today are the Primary Service Objective, the Marketing Circle, and $E \times KH = R$, which means "Energy times Know-How equals Results." All of these stemmed from the ten-second message: "Intelligently follow the directions of a superior [IFDOAS]."

Lesser speakers would have confused the issue and made the message an incitement for tighter control from above. The beginning of the lecture has that feel, as Sam talked about hierarchies and subordination. He even included an ancient Egyptian proverb: "To resist him that is set in authority is evil." The lecture, however, was no power grab; Sam intended to empower the individual.

Sam presented nothing new regarding his management philosophy, but he had to reach a broader audience—people who were new to the System—in a different forum. This is supported by Ralph Shivers, one of the many early management trainees who, when asked about the lecture, said, "I don't know why it got more notoriety, maybe it was more formalized. But this was an ongoing, continuing thing."

Sam himself knew his lecture was not for the early U-Haul System members. "I must caution the old-timers here not to get excited," he said. "What I have to say today will add little to past knowledge. Essentially all of this material is contained in existing publications of ARCOA. However, these publications cover a period of many years. Naturally, there exists some conflicts and confusion when viewed by more recent members of our organization."

Sam, as mentioned earlier, started by saying that the purpose of the conference was to transmit a ten-second message: "Intelligently follow the directions of a superior." He admitted the meeting was a bit extravagant for a ten-second message. He pointed out how at most meetings ninety percent of the time is spent entertaining those in attendance. "We intend to get ten seconds use out of 42,300 seconds," he said. That ten-second message, though, was one that involved a set of successful management principles U-Haul had relied on in the past. The lecture did not intend to say simply, "Do as you're told," but instead it stressed delegation and the principle that delegation allowed for: decision making "at the lowest level in the organization having the requisite competence, authority, and prestige" in order to best serve the customer. It is a simple enough concept on paper, but difficult to put into practice. By its very nature, it required independent thinkers and doers. They, however, could not strike out on their own and forget their roles within the System.

The early part of the lecture dealt with things such as the company hierarchy for the purpose of reacquainting the audience with the concept of organization. "[T]he very existence of man," said Sam, "is now and always has been dependent on the organization." Subordination is stressed because eventually the individual and the organization need to put their interests aside in order to fulfill the Primary Service Objective [PSO]: "To provide a better and better product and service to more and more people at a lower and lower cost."

"That is it," said Phil Schnee of the PSO. "Without that you have no organization."

Service was of primary importance in the lecture—doing for others. This was the essence of Logan Frank's lecture too, which, although it sounds like a lecture to be delivered to dealers, was directed to AFMs on how to best serve the dealers who served the customers throughout the U.S. In Sam's lecture, the PSO reminds System members that "the United States of America, permits us to exist and it would not long continue to do so if we did not put its interests first." Essentially, everyone served a subordinate role in any organization. Yet, in order to succeed, said Sam, "We must do this voluntarily and wholeheartedly if we are to succeed and prosper in this organization." He supplemented this point later when he defined what a "member" of the U-Haul System is: "A member of an organization is one who *accepts an obligation for the performance of certain functions [work] and discharges that obligation satisfactorily.*" This all led back to the extreme importance in observing and carrying out the Primary Service Objective.

It is a skillfully crafted argument. One of the company's charac-teristics in the early days was the independent spirit of working in the System. Fieldmen, as has been seen, often figured out the nuances of their job after a general briefing of responsibilities. The people in ARCOA saw avenues the company needed to take and they took them. But independence meant even stronger vigilance in carrying out the responsibilities of the job. All of this led to the Management Circle, which showed how each part of the organi-zation fed the other in a cyclical manner, which, if broken, wrecked the operations of the organization.

More importantly, though, the lecture stressed delegation. The hierarchies, the roles, subordination—they all boiled down to the concept of delegation. "As to those leaders directly under me," said Sam, "I exercise this right of decision and command just as they, in turn, exercise this right as to those subordinate to them. This right has been given to me by the owners of the organization who, in turn, received this right from the government of this country. I, in turn, delegate this right to my subordinates and so on down to the point of operative performance."

The two principles behind this, and what were of foremost importance in helping U-Haul succeed where other companies failed, were the principles of decentralized decision making and the principle of centralized support. Though these two princi-ples appear to stand in stark contrast to one another, they were certainly two elements that served U-Haul well from its inception.

Understanding these two principles means looking at Sam's differentiation between staff and line executives. A staff executive provides "a leadership of ideas and service. He has certain delegated rights of decision but no right of command except to his own staff subordinates." Line executives exercise "leadership of decision and command." Rental company presidents (formerly the rental company managers), AFMs, regional district managers, and Sam were line executives. Staff was engineering, accounting, advertising, research and development, and the secretarial pool.

The principle of centralized support required, "tighter headquarters control, *bigger staffs* [emphasis added]." ARCOA was to function more as a support organization, with a few line executives to whom the rest of the field reported. If the principle of delegation is applied then, rental company presidents and AFMs "have the authority needed to carry out the plans and policies of top management [at the ARCOA headquarters]."

"[Sam] kind of set this up," explained Schnee. "So basically, when we went back to our marketing companies or rental companies, we knew that these people [in Portland] were working for us. If it wasn't for the people in the field, there would be no ARCOA. There would be no people in Portland because [the field's] customer is the one who pays the paychecks for everybody in the organization."

This leads to the principle of decentralized decision making: "A decision should be made at the lowest level in the organization having the requisite competence, authority and prestige." Had there been extensive meddling in the daily operations of the marketing companies, right down to the AFMs, dealers would open at a snail's pace. Fieldmen had the authority to open dealers or to close them. This responsibility allowed AFMs to open dealers as quickly as possible and overwhelm rival dealers' lots with a saturation of U-Haul dealerships.

The system had, literally, human characteristics ingrained into its design, a nod to Sam's medical school days. "We have ARCOA," he said, "as the brain with the channels of communication carrying all significant information to the brain for study and a reasoned answer, then out again for action. Less complex communications stop at the spinal cord [rental companies] for a fast reply and quick action based on earlier experience [policy]."

Pat Crahan attested to Sam applying his policy of decision making at the lowest level, trusting his subordinates. Crahan was instructed by Sam to buy land to build a new shop in Oklahoma. "When we roomed together, I guess it was in Arkansas, it was after I bought the land and built the building. I said, 'Mr. Shoen, why don't you come back with me? We'll drive back. Then you can see the new building.' It was a big deal to me. He said, 'Okay I'll do it.' Got up the next morning, he said, 'No, I'm not going to go with you.' I said, 'Why not?' And this really made me feel good, he said, 'Pat, I know everything's okay in Oklahoma. I don't need to go look at your building. I need to go where the problems are.'"

Ultimately, Sam provided his audience with a formula for success, Energy times Know-How equals Results (E x KH = R). Energy and results are fairly easy to comprehend. The acquisition of KH, though, might be found in Sam's perception of the value of energy. During Pat Crahan's interview at the Skirvin Hotel in Oklahoma City, Sam asked what was more important: energy or knowledge. "I finally said 'energy,'" explained Pat, "because if you have enough energy you will find the knowledge [Know-How] and that happened to be his philosophy." In expending energy to acquire the KH, the individual is then led to people who know more about the subject at hand. Sometimes these people were in books, on which Sam relied—"into the books," so to speak. Other times KH came from people who had been around longer than the individual looking to gain more KH.

This search for knowledge is clearly demonstrated in Ron Frank's attempts to understand Sam's management bulletins. "I'd work and I'd work [to understand them]," he said, "and maybe I'd talk to Al Maynard—Texaco, or I'd talk to Nate Rossenwasser at an Amoco station and I'd just be talking to them as I'm out working on the equipment. And finally either someone would help me understand what the bulletin said or I'd hear a conversation from L.S."

Frank's and Crahan's stories validate Sam's explanation of where KH came from: "Intelligently following the directions of a superior." It led back to the organization and its hierarchies; that the people above were in charge because their experience warranted their being in that position. Seeking direction from a superior helped inform a subordinate and helped them accrue KH. Direction itself included delegation. Delegation allowed for subordinates to adapt as circumstances required without always having to seek approval from above.

The equation was popular for a long time with System members. Jim Shaw, in particular, loved it: "I don't see it in print much any more [sic], but E x KH = R was spread all over the organization. It was very important. If you learned that, just paid attention to that and nothing else, why . . . it got you going." While Shaw was with U-Haul, he put a lot of stock in the equation. "That in itself and the words that it stands for mean something to everybody. All you then have to do is adapt the communications that are out to their particular function. That can be done by way of *U-Haul News, Front Line,* any communications, John Dodds [retired executive vice president and current U-Haul Board member] and his meetings with people out in the field and ADVPs [area district vice presidents] and presidents repeating it. It can be in the very first interview of some new hire. It was a good message, and I think an awful lot of people got it. If you failed to bring it up, somebody brought it up to you when they saw it, like wearing the U-Haul tie clasp. The people saw it, and if they asked, boy, they got an explanation. And it was fun to explain. Any kind of tool like that is useful because the work ethic exists in an awful lot of people."

The lecture wrapped up with a final nod to the freedom afforded by the principle of centralization and the principle of decentralized decisions. "All of this is done by people," Sam said. "Therefore, we must realize that no person is physically, mentally or morally identical with any other person, that people are individuals and that they are most productive when doing what they want to do in a way they want to do it. The conflict between individual desire and group effectiveness is always present. We must continually strive to achieve economy and effectiveness while maintaining individual freedom."

"It unified the company," said Swanson, "because they were all speaking the same terms, the same policies, the same objectives." It brought *esprit de corps* to the System: those who attended saw that they were part of something larger than themselves. The lecture restated old policies in a different way for a new group of System members, and put everyone on the same page.

Not everyone jumped on board, which was probably one reason why Sam did the lecture: get everyone on the same page, and those who did not want to be there could leave. It was Sam's style, according to Jim Shaw. "L.S. Shoen was hard driving, meant business, gave opportunity and expected action," said Shaw. "Not everyone reacts to that stuff."

Ron Frank had one such person next to him during meetings outside the lectures, which Sam did not attend. "This guy would just bad-mouth L.S all week long," he said. "So at the final dinner, we had a banquet for everybody. So there sat L.S. and four of the guys who were traveling with him, and L.S. said, 'Well does anyone have anything they'd like to say or comments?' And of course, I mean, it got quieter than a church. That guy who had been bad-mouthing L.S. all week was sitting right next to me. I said, 'Hey, here's your opportunity to tell L.S. what you've been saying all week." L.S. erupted in laughter. His detractor slumped back into his chair and said nothing.

The '62 Lecture demonstrated the difference between U-Haul and the competition. "Nationwide and National both had a lot of damn good men," said Hap. "They had a lot of good people, but they really didn't have a nationwide organization. If you went to a meeting with those guys, which I've done, with the Nationwide guys, they argue about . . . I'll never forget this . . . they were arguing about who created their emblem. Who in the hell cares who created their emblem? But they'd argue like hell. They'd argue about stuff like that."

Ron Frank still carries his original copy of the lecture. Of the lecture he said, "The principles [Sam] talks about in there are timeless: *esprit de corps* and leadership. The principles that make life go. They make life go no matter which company you're in or what you're doing in life." Between the lecture and where the company was going, it was hard not to be excited about playing a role in something ready to explode. As Ron Frank remembered, "We were poised to push hard there in the '60s."

The views, philosophy and ideas expressed in the '62 Lecture were not simply advice to apply on the job. For Sam, it was something to live by. In April 1963, nearly a year after the lecture, Sam, Suzanne and their family were profiled on the front page of *The Daily Enterprise,* a paper in Riverside County, California. The article was titled, "He has a Special Slogan—and 70,000 trailers." The special slogan was IFDOAS. According to the article:

"IFDOAS is really Sam's slogan,' Suzanne explained, 'and it means intelligently follow the directions of a superior."

"It works for both our business and our home," Sam said. "Somebody up there is always thinking right along with you, so when the U-Haul trailer idea hit me, I just went ahead, and tried to intelligently follow His directions."

12

A HOUSEHOLD NAME

IN 1963, SAM was back to the basics. He did much of his work from his Palm Springs home, supplemented by frequent trips back to Portland. Tom O'Donnell ran things at ARCOA in Portland while Sam was in Palm Springs. ARCOA had a new home on Grand Avenue. In 1962, the headquarters on Hawthorne that once needed to scatter desks in the main work area to give the appearance that the company was large, was now bursting at the seams with one hundred employees. The new building had been a commercial laundry. After a renovation, it was an impressive three-story headquarters with a cafeteria inside. Sam, though, made Palm Springs his base. Logan Frank and Tom Safford had offices at Sam's Palm Springs home as well. The three would meet and work on innovations for the company. One of their tasks was a new marketing technique: a modular sign for U-Haul dealers.

Sam had once said, "I hope to make the rental trailer as common as Coca-Cola." Today, U-Haul is certainly synonymous with do-it-yourself moving. It is a household name. In order to become a household name, exceptional marketing efforts were needed to reach out to the American public so they would embrace the product and welcome it into their homes. In Palm Springs, Sam,

Logan and Safford were laying the groundwork for those unprecedented marketing efforts that would be a hallmark of the U-Haul Company throughout the '60s.

THAT LOGAN FRANK was involved in this effort is not surprising. Hap Carty called Logan "an innovator" in marketing for U-Haul. In his time at U-Haul, Logan not only was an expert fieldman; as the rental company manager in Florida and eventually Arizona-Nevada, he learned how to market his product well, to stand out from the competition. Sometimes he was a bit of a maverick when it came to marketing. For example, his ploy to rent trailers for two dollars from Florida to anywhere in the Northeast was enacted near Henry Bohannon's National Trailer Rental dealership, drawing the ire of Bohannon. Bohannon called Sam to complain about the crazy kid running the Florida area. Sam did not bat an eye, and the cheap rentals continued in order to move the product out of the sump of Florida.

At another point, Logan had another idea that shook up the System, "We were not sophisticated in keeping the trailers where they should go," remembered Logan. "It looked like if we didn't control it, all the trailers we owned, which wasn't that many in '56 and '57, would wind up in Florida, South Texas and California, particularly Florida. So they were coming in by droves down there, of those we had. So we had to do some kind of advertising. I was in Orlando, Florida, out on Colonial Boulevard in 1957. And this four-wheel tandem, five by twelve, rolled in with a new bright paint job on it and so forth. And I don't know why, but I looked at it and said, 'You know what? My sign just rolled in.'"

Logan contacted a local neon company to construct his new sign. The man he spoke with was a bit surprised. "I said, 'This tandem trailer here, I want to put it on a pole out front,'" explained Logan. "And he said, 'You mean you want a silhouette?' I said, 'No, I want to put that trailer right there. I want you to outline the U-Haul with orange neon. Then I want you to drill a hole in the bottom, put in a revolving unit, and I want it to revolve, that actual trailer.'

We put that trailer on a pole because Mr. Shoen had told me 'Get those trailers out of Florida, no matter what if you have to give them away.'"

The innovation worked fine, and Logan heard nothing about it until a year later when he received a U-Haul-O-Gram from Dick Wrublik. "He said, 'Logan, this trailer has not moved in over a year,' recalled Logan. "Please let me know if you can find it.' So I took a picture of it and I stapled it to the U-Haul-O-Gram, and I wrote, 'Dear Dick. This trailer has moved more than any trailer in the System the last year. It has never stopped moving, day and night.'"

A situation was rapidly brewing between people at ARCOA and Logan. Sam rushed down to Florida to assess the situation. He approved of what he saw and simply advised Logan to contact the Fleet Owner Department when setting up future displays so they would know which trailer he had put up on a pole.

Logan looked for and took any opportunity to market U-Haul. When clocks advertising U-Haul were available for dealers to put in their service stations, Logan looked beyond just dealers. "I just got the idea one day. I was getting my haircut, and they didn't have a clock on the wall. So I said, 'How'd you like to have a clock on the wall? I've got one in my truck out there.' [The barber] said, 'Okay put it up.' And bowling alleys. We put some in bowling alleys."

Duane Swanson, who was in charge of marketing, commented that many of the marketing ideas came from the field, from Logan in particular. "He was, and still is, very promotion minded, and he's a good leader," said Swanson. When reminded of Logan putting trailers on poles, though, Swanson hesitated. "He put trailers . . . it was one of the frustrating . . ." stammered Swanson, then he trailed off, laughing.

The trend caught on. A November 1959 *U-Haul News* features a picture of a trailer on the top of a tree painted orange to look like a pole. "What actually happened," the caption reads, "was that hurricane Hortense did the job of setting the van atop a tree." The caption ends with "[Ed. Note: Now get my trailer down off of there, and cut out this foolishness, fellows!]."

"Duane and I had a lot of fun over the years together," said Logan. "Duane, he referred to my trailers and trucks on a pole as 'gauche.'"

"It was a way of advertising," explained Dee Frank. "At that time, we couldn't do anything else. Duane was one who, if a building was built, he'd want a [small sign] in a corner somewhere. Logan wanted flashing lights, banners, and all of it."

Toward the end of 1963, Logan was heading up the Arizona-Nevada company. Asthma and nasal problems prompted the move to drier weather. His knack for eye-catching displays for trailers did not end, though. "He would put a trailer in the back of a pickup truck or on a flatbed," said Swanson. "I gave him a hard time about that, figuring that it was corny."

Logan, however, was determined. The trailers in the pickups were once again used to set U-Haul apart from the competition. It also helped to reinforce the notion that being a U-Haul dealer was a great opportunity for service station owners. "We sent those all over the country," explained Logan, "and we'd open dealers with those at full-service service stations. And we'd have a grand opening!"

Even Duane Swanson bought into the idea: "But bless his heart; he was that dedicated and promotion minded. I thought it was kind of corny, and he thought I was dumb because I thought it was corny. But it worked."

Any disagreement was tempered by Swanson's attitude toward disputes. "We would disagree, but we were never disagreeable," he recalled.

"Duane and I were good friends," affirmed Logan—their long working relationship in U-Haul attests to this. "It was just . . . Duane, he was a little more polished than I was."

Regardless, when the idea of a modular sign became a potential marketing tool, Logan was consulted and worked alongside Sam and Tom Safford, who in turn all worked with Duane Swanson, who was in Portland.

The concept of a modular sign led to the final alteration in the U-Haul logo. "I changed the logo in the '60s," explained Swanson. "The U-Haul was changed from this italic style to a 'U' a large 'U,' and an attachment. The hyphen was attached to the 'H' in a bolder, cleaner typeface. And that was done on purpose so that when we did a modular sign you didn't have to have six panels; you had to have five." Economical and effective; exactly what Sam called for in the '62 Lecture. That example demonstrates just how acutely aware everyone was regarding "E and E," even down to the design of the logo. The first modular sign would appear in 1966.

For many years the Marketing Department was comprised of only one man, Duane Swanson, who hired staff artists to assist him. Duane, however, ran himself ragged performing his duties as the head of Marketing, artist, graphic designer, photographer—the list was endless. But in 1962, his department was expanding, and taking on more responsibility. His work helped the company grow to something the first person in charge of advertising, Ray Robbins, never expected. "By then, it sort of became a giant corporation," said Robbins. "And to be part of that was sort of a thrill for me because we were definitely nationwide."

Robbins had taken his second leave of absence to attend art school in Los Angeles. During that time, Sam sent money to Robbins to help him with living expenses, which was an investment of sorts. Robbins came back to do cartooning again and discovered U-Haul truly was a household name. Not only was it a household name, but it was in front of millions of Americans every day during their breakfasts. U-Haul placed toys in the boxes of Trix Cereal, a product of General Mills. It was a major victory for U-Haul and its Marketing Department. When asked if it was like being on a Wheaties box, Robbins said, "Yeah it was. It was sort of fun walking down a grocery store aisle and seeing something that you were a part of."

The June 1962 issue of *U-Haul News* announced this windfall for the company. The promotion included one plastic frame trailer. On the frame, three cutout designs on the back of the box could be attached to the frame. The trailer could then be attached, according to the television ad, "to a model car. Like the model cars you can purchase from these other 'big G' cereals." The campaign included sixteen television commercials that would reach forty-eight million homes. Grocery stores would be provided with full-sized U-Haul trailers to act as "a portable display bin."

"Everybody wanted to buy Trix then," recalled Bill Carpenter. "You could hardly find Trix when they came out with that on the box. Hard to tell why people wanted U-Haul, but we were kind of glad they did."

"It was interesting that in 1962, they would think U-Haul was pretty big in those days. Worth putting on a box," said Swanson.

There was also an unspoken message that benefited U-Haul: If the manufacturers of the food parents served their children at breakfast thought highly of U-Haul, then perhaps it was a tacit endorsement of the company's equipment in regard to the safety of their family when moving.

Toy U-Haul trailers had been around since 1960. It is odd to think of them now as ideal gifts, but they proved quite popular. Dealers sold them, and they could be ordered through the *U-Haul News*. Many U-Haul members gave the toys as gifts to family and extended family on holidays and birthdays. "I'd always buy them as they came out," said Jacque Hedwall, "and then I'd have them at home so that when [nieces and nephews] came and visited they'd play. Half the time I lost [the toys] all because they'd be crying and screaming and bawling because they didn't want to leave the toy behind. I'd have to send it with them so they'd go home. I still have some."

"It was an exciting thing for the company," said Swanson, who still has the original car and trailer set made by Nylint, "because here we are a little growing company and all of sudden we have a toy made after us."

The toy makers would either contact U-Haul or, if a new product was coming out, U-Haul would contact them to create a new toy fashioned after the new product. "That's more exposure because that's on the shelves of a toy store," explained Swanson. The toys targeted a demographic that most often used the trailers: families with young children.

* * *

THESE LANDMARK MARKETING successes could not have been accomplished without the establishment of A&M Associates, an in-house marketing company for ARCOA. Duane Swanson acknowledged the letters had a double meaning. When asked what A&M stands for, he initially said, "Advertising and Marketing," but when asked if it meant Anna Mary, a broad smile covered his face. "And that, too," he said, nodding. "That was subtle, but that's true."

The motivation to launch A&M came from the do-it-yourself spirit of U-Haul. Prior to A&M, U-Haul had to retain an outside advertising company. Sam and Swanson saw a problem in the process. Generally, for an advertisement to be sold, companies hired agencies to do the advertisement and buy space in magazines or newspapers or billboards. Fifteen percent of the cost went to the agency. "We had a couple agencies at first," said Swanson "and then we thought, 'Wait a minute! They're making fifteen percent for doing the work we're already doing.' [The ad agencies] just gave it to the telephone company and made fifteen percent. So why not do it ourselves?"

BUOYED BY THE success of the Trix campaign, U-Haul lost no momentum heading into 1963. The company launched another advertising campaign, this time with *Life* magazine between May and September. "That's really the big time," recalled Ray Robbins. "Duane and I went back to New York for some meeting about it. And to me, I really felt I was in big-time advertising when we actually got to show up in *Life* magazine. Looking back on it now, it was probably a relatively low-budget ad by *Life* standards because they're used to big full-page, full-color, sometimes double-page ads. The main ones we ran in *Life* were a single column, maybe two color. But to us it was big time. It had such a gigantic circulation and it was just such a well-known magazine. So dollars-and-cents-wise, I'm not sure if it paid off, but it was sure great trying it."

Sam generally left Swanson alone to do his own work, which Swanson preferred, as most artists do. But on occasion, Sam would offer his input on marketing. "I'd have L.S. Shoen correct stuff," recalled Swanson. "Well, L.S. Shoen didn't know graphics very well. He would put on a sign, a billboard for example, he'd put on about fifty words of copy. That was probably the most frustrating thing, a lot of copy. If you ever did an ad for him, it was full of copy, and nobody's going to read that. A billboard, for example, should have no more than seven words. Four or five are good to make the point. But twenty or thirty words, forget it. Many times we'd end up with a thing with a lot of words in it, especially the Yellow Pages ads." Swanson, however, was never bothered by that. "That's all right," he said. "That's their prerogative. I'm a staff person. I advise. A line person makes the decisions. I have to recognize that."

In terms of working with Sam on cutting down the words, Ray Robbins, said, Swanson probably won the day most of the time. "Duane was a very good editor, so he was able to do that." Ray Robbins said Swanson was perfect to head up Marketing. "I have to give Duane Swanson a lot of credit because I thought he was extremely professional. He has a very good eye for advertising." Robbins' time with A&M and Duane improved him as well: "I can say that when I started, I was a hobbyist. After [art] school, I became a professional. And I was not just a professional artist, but I was a professional advertising person too."

FOR ALL THEIR work in making U-Haul a household name, A&M apparently could not break through to one important home: the White House. "We had a dealership at Andrews Air Force Base. That was the base that President Kennedy used," Phil Schnee said. "We had trailers and trucks there on that base. Just about an hour or so before takeoff, the President would plan to come through there with his entourage to get on *Air Force One*, they would go by that gas station [dealer] we had there. And they would call us. They'd say, 'Get your equipment out of here. The President's coming through here.' So we would have to drop what we were doing, go down there with a couple of field rigs and move that equipment out of there until the President went through. Now if he was going to be gone a few days we could put it back, and everything was fine, until about an hour or so before he was scheduled to land. They'd call us up again. So we did this several times until we finally convinced these people that the President doesn't really care. He's got other things on his mind besides U-Haul trailers and trucks."

U-Haul was affected by and even played a part in some of the political turbulence at the time. Phil Schnee oversaw field operations in Washington, DC during the Cuban Missile Crisis in 1962, an event that moved the Cold War between the Soviet Union and the United States to the brink of nuclear war. The Soviet Union, allied with Cuba, began a military buildup on the Caribbean island located 90 miles off the Florida coast. Part of this buildup included medium-range missiles that had a range of 1,100 miles, which was "easily sufficient to hit major population centers in the United States. Later revelations also indicated that the Soviets had in readiness nine tactical missiles with nuclear warheads."

"Somebody was ready to push the button," said Schnee. "When this happened, I called my field reps and told them to stay home. 'Don't go to work today. This is not a place to be.' Some of that stuff was aimed at Washington, DC. I was not more than ten miles outside of DC, our little office we had there. So we told everybody to stay at home. Don't go to work until this is over with. It was a little touchy there."

The country avoided mutually assured destruction. But in 1963, U-Haul participated in an assault on the Eastern Bloc countries. The United States Commerce Department had agreed to participate at the International Trade Fair in Zagreb, Yugoslavia. The U.S. was anxious to show off its new pride, the interstate highway system. Perhaps it was a bit of karma for the slights at Andrews, but U-Haul was chosen to represent the "trailer trend." More than likely it was recognition of U-Haul as the leader in the truck- and trailer-rental industry. The government's request for U-Haul to participate mentioned "that moving with trailers was an integral part to America's mobile economy." To a nation whose citizens faced heavy travel restrictions, the idea of packing up and moving with ease wherever a car and the U-Haul trailer could go probably sparked as many dreams of freedom overseas as it had enabled at home.

Vin Kiley escorted the trailer to the communist nation. President Tito of Yugoslavia viewed the display. Over a million people viewed the display that "was a U-Haul first . . . the honor of representing what is now an important American tradition . . . do-it-yourself moving with trailers."

THE CUBAN MISSILE Crisis cost U-Haul a valuable System member. The draft notice Henry Kelly knew was coming arrived in 1962. He had been scheduled to take the reins of a manufacturing plant on Long Island, but instead he proudly fulfilled his duty over the next two years. Upon his return, he, Frank Lyons at Warrington Equipment Manufacturing and Bill Jakubek of Falls Manufacturing spearheaded the proliferation of trucks in U-Haul fleets.

By 1964, trucks were an essential product produced by the manufacturing plants. Truck manufacturing did not involve building the actual truck chassis. The plants took delivery of truck bodies from automobile manufacturers. At U-Haul plants, workers built van bodies from kits, which they attached to the truck chassis. In 1964, plants turned out Ford trucks, a departure from the original Dodges. "Dodge Corporation was the one that we started putting the van body on. That became a little bit of a drawback for us," explained Henry Kelly. "Dodge did not have a good network as far as the customers if they needed to stop along the way and get something fixed. And this is the reason that we went with Ford. It wasn't that everybody felt that Ford was a better product. It was that Ford had a better dealer organization than anybody."

The number of trucks and the priority given to them in manufacturing was remarkable considering the company had introduced them only five years earlier. Now, in 1964, they were rolling out of the plants. "I don't know that anybody had the foresight to know how big it would get, the trucks," said Frank Lyons. "It grew, and grew pretty quickly."

Dick Wrublik noted that the growth was spurred by changing corporate laws. "We had a situation that set the tone for the next twenty years," said Wrublik. "This program of accelerated depreciation investment credit was about to expire. It was helping people [who had invested in the Fleet Owner Program] too much. It [the law change] happened in '64 or 65. I was trying to really expand and catch the other competitors off guard and have our truck deals solidified before they knew what hit 'em. We went out and bought a two-year supply of trucks. Firm orders: People to buy it; people to build it. Everything was all done. And we pulled it off before they changed the law, so we were able to continue on for two years with maximum production, getting full investment credit and accelerated depreciation for all that equipment . . . and that was millions of dollars [in savings for U-Haul and fleet owners]. That was an important deal, and it worked two ways because we had such a big order we got a special discount from the manufacturer, and everything, all the way through to the increased investors. We didn't have any trouble worrying about paying for it because there was a tremendous increase of rentals which made the rental companies and ARCOA very profitable."

Hap credited Lyons and Kelly for spearheading this initiative: "[Lyons] and Henry Kelly ran our two primary truck-production plants. And if you put all the trucks, bumper to bumper, that came out of their two plants, there wouldn't be enough room between [Phoenix] and LA for them."

LYONS WAS HAP'S brother-in-law, who went out east, when Hap was there to start his career in U-Haul. He did field work in the New Jersey area before transferring to Willow Grove. "The opportunity came up to get into the product area of the business," said Lyons, "and I thought I'd like that more. Basically, I went down and ran the repair shop in Willow Grove for awhile to get some kind of product knowledge, and that's about the time we were really starting to build trucks. I helped build some of the kits that we originally bought. Then we opened up Warrington and went into business building trucks and trailers."

Henry Kelly's education in the field of truck manufacturing had been a bit more difficult. In 1960, he was put in charge of the first trailer-manufacturing plant in Canada. "I hired a crew of about eighteen people. I hired a used-car salesman for a manager, but he had managerial experience. And we were on a roll to do exactly what the plan was," explained Henry. "Most of our materials were stamped in Pennsylvania for this trailer. The markings, decals, were made in Pennsylvania. Everything had to come through customs, and when it came through customs we had to pay customs taxes. So the cost of this trailer was very expensive compared to its cost in the states. L.S. Shoen called me up, after we were running full blast, and said, 'After this run . . . it's too expensive to build equipment up in there. I only want you to build that group and then close it up.'"

Henry was pretty distraught, and he called Hap for some advice: "He said, 'Henry tomorrow's Friday. Here's my suggestion. Get everyone together and explain to them what's going on. They'll understand. They'll rally around the flag and try to get this done. In the meantime, try to find them work.' I took Hap's advice, and got everyone together and told them we were going to close the place, and I'd appreciate it if they stuck around, and I'd try to find them jobs and so forth. Come Monday morning, only six guys showed up. Now I knew I was in trouble because I still had something like thirty trailers to build. Needless to say, by the end of the week, no one was left. So it took me about three months to build the other thirty trailers." It was an ignominious introduction to the world of manufacturing.

Henry had other concerns though. A year later, he was drafted.

When Kelly returned, Hap had a surprise for him. "He basically waited until I got out of the service to offer me the job as head of the Long Island manufacturing plant," Kelly recalled.

Kelly used the plant's location to name the new plant. "It was in a town on Long Island called Holbrook, and I went down to city hall to see if anybody had ever used Holbrook Manufacturing," said

Henry. "They hadn't. So I helped incorporate it under Holbrook Manufacturing. There were some good reasons to call it the local name. You seemed to get the council to do more for you when you went up in front of them. They would help you out as far as maybe [with] some zoning. We had to not only build the equipment, but we had to store it. We had to have big trucks come and get it. Big trucks delivered our parts. Not every community appreciates this all the time. They were kind of proud. They liked the type of work we were doing. You have to realize, in those days, Long Island did not encourage business on the island."

WHILE KELLY WAS setting up Holbrook, Warrington had a more dubious start. "Warrington's a good example of how decentralized authority was in the organization," said Hap. "That building covers about an acre. That's a pretty good-size building for U-Haul. When the red-iron was going up, the steel structure, L.S. came back there, and he didn't know we were building it. He got upset about it, too. And he said, 'You won't lay another brick in Pennsylvania until every rental company has a headquarters.' I said, 'Sam, you just bought a building department.' And Vin Kiley ran it, and we built headquarters."

"Hap came in one day," said Vin, "with a napkin from Howard Johnson from Memphis, Tennessee, and he drew out a sketch of a building, a floor plan. Hap said, 'Why don't you lay one out and see what you can do with it?' I did the drawings. The whole thing, I built it. We built about twenty of those around the country. I was the general contractor in a sense. I went out and got the bids and eventually got Charlie Otto working for me. We did the drawings, we did our bids, and we shot the jobs. That way we could build at a lower cost and get a little more quality. They're still standing today. Pretty nice little buildings."

"Those old rental company headquarters," said Hap, "Vin Kiley was the brains on getting that done." Once the headquarters were built, the plans for Warrington Truck Manufacturing's development were ready to go.

* * *

WARRINGTON, LOCATED ONLY eight miles up PA-611 from Willow Grove, might have seemed redundant as another manufacturing plant in such a close proximity; but the rental industry was outgrowing Willow Grove's manufacturing capabilities. "It was an old building," said Lyons of Willow Grove, "pretty well crammed in. Little if any parking space outside. Warrington was a brand-new building. First building was one hundred feet by two hundred feet, twenty thousand square feet. Then we built lean-tos off the side, which expanded it. We were on a total of ten acres in '64. Then in '65, we required two other buildings. So it was a far better situation as far as running a plant. We had room. We had a new facility, new equipment. Willow Grove would have been more difficult, but it was a different operation." The industry was moving fast. Willow Grove had been the jewel of manufacturing within the System since 1954, but ten years later, it had served its purpose. The trucks were taking over. The new space at Warrington had plenty of people occupying it. "At that time we were building trucks, trailers and doing repair, all in the same building," said Lyons.

Not long after this, Henry Kelly was sent to Novi, Michigan, to set up yet another plant. These two plants would provide the U-Haul System with the mass of trucks that Hap described.

"IF I WAS going to say something about Frank, I'd say the same thing about Henry," said Hap. "They both, somehow, attracted top people and kept them in the organization. They were both productive, happy, proud."

Henry Kelly's ability to attract top people was rooted in the early star-crossed misfortunes in Canada. "[Hap] was right," said Henry. "You always want to be truthful with people, but you better be ready for the outcome." Henry's straightforward attitude with his workers helped in building a quality group of people at Novi.

* * *

AT THE CLOSE of 1964, U-Haul was the standard bearer in do-it-yourself moving. The structure was in place to ensure forward progress and continued development to adapt to a changing environment. It was the principle of the marketplace in Sam's '62 Lecture. "We must give the consumer what he wants, when he wants it, where he wants it, at a price he is willing to pay," he said. "Otherwise, U-Haul will no longer be of service to the organization of society as a whole." By 1964, though, the company had become exactly what Sam had hoped. It was a name as recognizable as Coke or Kleenex. "The name U-Haul really has high recognition. It's a brand name," said Duane Swanson. "That's an important thing: That the brand name is highly recognizable. I'd say ninety percent or more of people know what U-Haul is."

The story of U-Haul does have some things in common with other innovations that are now woven into the fabric of society and ingrained in the postwar history of the United States, companies like McDonald's, Holiday Inn, and Levitt and Sons. Many other, less fortunate companies sprang up at this time; most failed. Those that succeeded did so through persistence and keeping service as their primary objective.

According to David Halberstam's book *The Fifties,* Ray Kroc, founder of McDonald's, was annoyed by his competition because "they were out to make money . . . not hamburgers and perform a service." He even sounded like Sam when it came to the notion of persistence: "Nothing in the world can take the place of persistence. Genius will not. Unrewarded genius is almost a problem. Talent will not. The world is filled with unsuccessful men of talent. Education will not. The world is filled with educated derelicts." Compare that to Sam's take on a Jefferson aphorism: "I believe in luck. The harder I work, the luckier I get." Or to distill it further: E x KH = R.

Halberstam's book, like many other books on U.S. history discussing the postwar years, speaks at great length about innovations that helped America grow and expand as a nation, but it never once talks about U-Haul trailers. Yet the trailer was one of the most vital tools American families used in the 1950s and early '60s.

"If you get something that people use, a lot of people use," said Hap while talking about trailers, "but they use it very infrequently, it has a long life, has the ability to appreciate—that's an ideal rental product."

"[U-Haul trailers] were built tough," said Duane Swanson. "And durable, and through the years they found out [U-Haul] had to do that. In the rental business that stuff takes tremendous abuse."

U-Haul helped Americans move. Its products helped serve that "noble function," to move, of which Kerouac wrote in *On the Road.* U-Haul trailers were simple and functional. They served Americans who *needed* them. As Duane Swanson said, "[U-Haul] is a blue-collar labor service—somebody who's going to do it himself. If you got big bucks then you'll hire somebody to move it for you. This is for the people who had no other way of moving their goods."

The success of U-Haul trailers allowed the company to fulfill its Primary Service Objective: "To provide a better and better product and service to more and more people at a lower and lower cost," by introducing trailers into the rental business . . . all of it done to give more Americans the opportunity to move their families in a safe, economical manner.

"I think that's another reason I liked the company . . . because I liked what the company was doing," said Jerry Ayres. "The little guy didn't have money. He had to move himself and this was the cheapest way for him to go. It was an easy way. When he got someplace, he didn't have to wait for the truckers to bring it in."

Simply put: the essence of the trailers, what they were and what they did, fulfilled a noble function. Hap put it into a perspective that reflects the humility of the company and how it fit into the American scene from 1945–1964, "Ford built the cars," he said. "The government built the roads. We built the trailers."

"Interesting company, interesting time, wouldn't have missed it for the world," remembered Ralph Shivers. "The best analogy that comes to mind, that I continually think of, is that going to work for U-Haul, when I did, when—I don't know—whether there was twenty or forty people, certainly not more than that, [it] was like going to work for Henry Ford when he was in that garage, and then staying with him and seeing that organization grow to a mass of dealers."

EPILOGUE: THIS DAY

PAT CRAHAN'S FIRST few weeks as the rental company president of U-Haul of Oklahoma-Arkansas were rough. Some of the employees at his company tried to run him off. He stood firm, and replaced those people. He took his lumps doing it, though, all while he was trying to learn a business that was entirely foreign to him. Shortly after Pat Crahan's interview at the Skirvin hotel, he hit the road with veteran System member Bert Miller, who had parted ways with U-Haul sometime before. Miller was looking for a new job and Sam, as a favor and probationary rehire, asked Miller to train Crahan. Pat and Bert serviced trailers as they drove to meet Sam in Tennessee. "They had a companywide meeting in Memphis, Tennessee," Crahan remembered. "Bert had told me, 'We're starting work at six in the morning, Pat.' I said, 'Okay.' So we started work at six in the morning: *work*. We were working on trailers and such, changing bearings and stuff. 'You're president, but you got to do all this work,' he said. 'Okay with me,' I said. I didn't know anything about [trailers]. He trained me pretty well. And we worked dealers all the way over." Miller made sure the two followed Bob Clarke's memo to fieldmen about living on three dollars a day. "That's what we did all the way from Oklahoma. It took about three days. So we stopped and bought an apple and lunch meat and whatnot, and cheese.

"As we got closer and closer to Tennessee, he got softer. Finally on the last day, as we were driving in, the last few hundred miles, he told me flatly, 'Pat I've been trying to run you off ever since I got here. Doesn't look like I'm going to be successful.' Then he was very honest. 'Pat,' he tells me, 'I don't have any money. I've been out of a job. I only have enough money to pay my motel bill. If I don't get a job with U-Haul, I'm really going to be out of luck.'" Pat paused for a moment. "I don't think I've told anybody that."

Given all the turmoil and upheaval, Pat had reservations about his new job by the time he arrived in Memphis. "The conference was over, and I was just very quiet in the conference. We had break-fast together [on the last day] and some of the guys were staying. I went out to get my car, and Sam followed me out. I was getting in the car, and he said, 'Pat, how are things going?' I said, 'Mr. Shoen, if I had known at the time you hired me what I know now, I would not have taken the job.' And he just died laughing. He had a great laugh. He patted me on the back and said, 'That's why I didn't tell you. I knew about all those things. If I had told you about them, you wouldn't have taken the job.' I said, 'I don't quit.' He said, 'Okay, good for you,' and he sent me off. "

As for Bert Miller, Sam nonchalantly asked Pat, "Bert teach you a lot?"

"I told him yes. I never said anything against him," Pat said. "We became really good friends. He did get a job. He was put in as pres-ident of Georgia. So everything worked out okay for him."

Opportunity and second chances were two key enticements U-Haul had to offer young men and women in America at that time. The company drove the unmotivated away. But even the dedicated needed a break. "I did leave once," Jacque Hedwall recalled. "I took a leave of absence. Went to work for a while at a plywood company, it lasted two weeks and I came back. I was never comfortable [at the plywood company]. I always thought: [U-Haul] is the only job I ever had, so I've got to give something else a try to see if this is really what I want to stay at. They were plywood exporters at the time. I guess there was just nobody to relate to. It was one of those things where the money wasn't bad. The job probably would have been okay, but it was just me. It was very cold. I just decided it wasn't for me."

Others felt the need to test the waters elsewhere. Later in his career, Logan Frank tired of staff work but was not put back out into the field; he took a leave of absence, although he thought it was more permanent than Sam. "My parents lived in Canyon, Texas, and so I said, I'm going to go out there and do something else," Logan said. "I didn't know what I was going to do—sell spark plugs to service stations. I wanted action. I didn't want a desk job. I got over there, and my [U-Haul] paycheck kept coming. About two months later, I called L.S. I said, 'Mr. Shoen,' 'Hey, Logan how are you doing?' he said. 'I'm still getting my paycheck.' 'I know it. Don't worry about it. I'm busy. I'm in a meeting. Don't worry about your check.' My checks kept coming. So I never really did quit. So then about four months later, he called me one day. He said, 'Hey, what are you doing?" I said 'Well, I'm not doing much today.' He said, 'Will you run up to Kansas City for me and see what's going on in that office up there and straighten things out?'" A soft, demure smile crossed Logan's face. "What are you going to say? That shows a lot. He could've said, 'He left, to heck with him, bye.' I've always appreciated that. And I've never thought about, since that day, of ever leaving again."

Some people believed U-Haul was not in their long-term future. "When I started on this thing, I figured—get another experience. I'd spend two years then I'd take off and find something else," recalled Jerry Ayres. "That was almost forty-one years ago." (Ayres retired in 1998.)

At times, the competition tried to lure U-Haul System members like Logan away: "I don't live for money. Twice Hertz offered me a lot of money to come work for them. Wanted me to go to Chicago. I didn't want to do it."

"I didn't want to move to Chicago," said Dee wryly. "Like I said, our blood was orange, loyal. I knew he wouldn't be happy."

The nature of U-Haul in the first twenty years drove away the weak and attracted the strong; a fact that still amazes Hap. "I don't know how in the hell we got all those good men," he said. "I don't like to name anybody because we had so many. If you name five, you leave out a thousand that should be named."

Part of this success might have been from many System members making U-Haul not just a job, but a lifestyle. "I think I've gone around this world twice with a trailer behind that car," Helen Shoen said. "In fact, it was kind of funny. One daughter, who was pretty young then to remember much of anything, told me, 'I can remember one time when Dad was unhitching the trailer, and I cried because I thought there was something wrong with the car.' We just didn't usually do that. It was part of our life, and I guess when we would travel all through the country I would say, 'Okay, girls, sit up and be proud: There's our bread and butter,' every time we would see a U-Haul [trailer]."

On vacations, the company was never far from System members' minds. "When we went on our honeymoon, you know what we did?" asked Vivian Shaw, recounting the trip she and Jim took. "We counted up trailers and trucks on the competitors' lots. That's how we spent our honeymoon: doing U-Haul work. I think all U-Haulers were a little bit nuts. They all went and did things for U-Haul on their own time, and didn't think anything about it."

Even in retirement, the early System members could not let go of their responsibility to the company. "Phil [Schnee] and I were vacationing two or three years ago," remembered Ron Green. "We were in Utah. And we were down in St. George, and we're driving around and there's this FS open trailer. This guy was doing lawn gardening. He was driving around with this FS behind him. So it looked like it should still be in U-Haul, and we checked it, and it was. So we called the fleet owner. They found out that it was supposed to be recovered. It hadn't yet. The guy was supposed to turn it in. [U-Haul] said, 'Well, we got a guy in the area who will be over to see him. How come you're calling me? A lot of people don't bother.' I said, 'Number One, I'm a fleet owner.' I said, 'You know what? Right now, you are talking to ninety years of U-Haul personnel' because Phil had forty-five years and I had forty-five years. And I said, 'So we got ninety years of U-Haul experience here, and we want to know why our trailer ain't back out there working.'"

This was a loyalty possessed by people who woke up and saw their job as fun, despite difficult times or obstacles to success. The early familial feel, the Fleet Owner Program and the *esprit de corps* instilled by Sam made U-Haul more than a company. To people like Ron Green, Phil Schnee, Jacque Hedwall, Hap Carty, Vivian Shaw and all the rest, U-Haul was a family they enjoyed seeing grow.

"We've always produced a quality product, and we've always taken our customers as Number One," said Ron Green. "Everything we do, we do top notch. We do it the best. That's why we succeeded. I look at it this way: I've never been rich, but I've worked for forty-five years. I've never been out of work. But we're retired, we're comfortable, we're doing what we want to do, and U-Haul helped us do it. Like Sam told me before, 'Never give up something you've got until you find something better.' And I've never found anything better, and I think a lot of people would find the same thing."

Phil Schnee agreed with Green. "People that start out today see that there are a lot of us out there who put in our time. We did it. We helped build this thing," he said. "It's a good feeling. When I did my yearbook, when they asked what you did in your life, I said 'I helped build U-Haul.' What little work I did, I helped build. It's a 'we' organization."

Vivian Shaw concurred. "I think it was the people," she said, "and Sam's leadership."

"I don't know how to explain it," said Hap. "I'm really proud of what U-Haul did. We did it. When I say 'we,' I mean *we*. Sam was certainly without question the dynamic force, the original dynamic force. But we had dynamic forces all over the country. Let me tell you something about U-Haul. One of the reasons it lasted is that we had a bunch of men that were afraid of nothing. We didn't have to run around begging for a job. The average guy that you've got in your book, they're somebody to deal with. They're going to starve to death [in order to get the job done]; they're going to be productive one way or another. That's just the way they are."

From 1945–1964, opportunity was truly limitless both for the company and System members. "I think one of the things, why a lot of people who worked liked their supervisors, was that there were so many opportunities for advancement," Hap said. "If you wanted to be a rental company president, well . . . what's holding you back?"

Henry Kelly, the young high school graduate from Philadelphia, was one such man who wasn't held back. He ran a large production plant and has held various executive positions within the company. He saw the country and helped build an industry. "If I had to do it all over again, I would fill out an application with U-Haul," said Kelly. "We've had our ups and downs, like any other company, but sixty years . . . everybody's proud of that. Even my brother, who is younger and retired now, he did spend twenty years with the company, he will make the same comment that he never worked with any company like U-Haul. And he's never developed friendships like he developed here. The interesting thing about that is that most of us made our friends after we came on the job."

Ron Green agreed, and at Willow Grove those friendships led to better innovations. "I'll tell you one thing about the Engineering, Research and Development Department," said Ron. "Sometimes after work a lot of us would get together and just brainstorm a little bit. We'd say, 'Here's the problem.' And one guy would say, 'Well maybe we can do this.' That would stimulate someone else's thinking. That would stimulate someone else. Pretty soon we'd come up with a solution, and then we'd go do it."

BEFORE HE PENNED the *Declaration of Independence,* Thomas Jefferson wrote one final appeal to the British crown, in an effort to help the king understand the differences between the American colonists and the people of England. "[O]ur ancestors," explained Jefferson "before their emigration to America, were the free inhabitants of the British dominions in Europe, and possessed *a right, which nature has given to all men, of departing from the country in which chance, not choice, has placed them, of going in quest of new habitations, and of there establishing new societies, under such laws and regulations as to them shall seem most likely to promote public happiness* [emphasis added]."

There is an immense pride these people have in what they accomplished during these first twenty years. This pride is rooted in something deeper than just building an industry. It's a pride derived from helping people in America fulfill the natural right that Jefferson and Kerouac believed in. This pride helped them to see their jobs not merely as work, but as something more personally fulfilling. As Logan Frank said, "It's important to have fun on the job because life is short. Yesterday, I was twenty-four years old, figuratively speaking . . . just yesterday. I'd do it all over again if I could, but I can't. The trick is . . ." He trailed off, and took a considered, contemplative pause. "You know," he continued, "I've known people, they live in a perpetual fog of regretful yesterdays and fearful, catastrophic tomorrows. And they never have lived *this* day."

BIBLIOGRAPHY

U-Haul Co. Corporate Publications:
"How A Dealer Can and Will Do His Job"
"We're Asking for It"
AMERCO *World,* January 8, 1971
Annual Meeting of the Stockholders of U-Haul Co. January 20. 1951
Regular Meeting of the Board of Directors of the U-Haul Co. November 3, 1948
Regular Meeting of the Board of Directors of the U-Haul Co. February 2, 1949
U-Haul News, November 1954
U-Haul News, November 1955
U-Haul News, August 1956
U-Haul News, October 1956
U-Haul News, December 1956
U-Haul News, October 1957
U-Haul News, April 1959
U-Haul News, November 19, 1959
U-Haul News, November 1959
U-Haul News, June 1960
U-Haul News, September 1960
U-Haul News, November 1960
U-Haul News, July 1961
U-Haul News, September/October 1993

Books:

Brinkley, Alan. *The Unfinished Nation*. New York: Knopf, 1993.

Gibran, Kahlil. *The Prophet*. New York: Knopf, 1923.

Halberstam, David. *The Fifties*. New York: Random House, 1994.

Jefferson, Thomas. "A View of the Rights of British America." *The Portable Thomas Jefferson*. Ed. Merrill D. Peterson. New York: Penguin, 1975. 3–21.

John XXIII, Pope. *Mater et Magistra: Encyclical Letter of His Holiness John XXIII, a Re-evaluation of the Social Question in the Light of Christian Teaching*. New York: Paulist Press, 1961.

Kerouac, Jack. *On the Road*. 1957. Introduction Ann Charters London: Penguin, 1991.

Patterson, James T. *Grand Expectations*. Oxford: Oxford U.P., 1996.

Shoen, L. S. *You and Me*. Phoenix: AMERCO, 1980.

Weingroff, Richard F. "Zero Milestone, Washington D.C." *U.S. Department of Transportation, Federal Highway Administration*. 7 May 2005. 10 Oct. 2006 <http://www.fhwa.dot.gov/infrastructure/zero.htm>.

Transcripts from interviews conducted by U-Haul in 1988:

Duane Swanson, 1988

Helen Shoen, 1988

Jim Shaw, 1988

Mike Morelli, 1988

Tom O'Donnell, 1988

Vin Kiley, 1988

Vivian Shaw, 1988

Other:

Wilcoxon, Joan. *The Daily Enterprise*. April 20, 1963. B-2A

"Navy V-12 Program." *U.S. Navy Memorial*. 1 Jan. 2006. 18 October 2006 <http://www.lonesailor.org/v12history.php>.

NOTES

CHAPTER 1: The Reluctant Businessman
In this chapter, I reference or quote from Alan Brinkley's *The Unfinished Nation* (635); L.S. Shoen's *You and Me* (2–5, 11, 33, 41, 89–90, 92–94, 183); Richard Weingroff's article "Zero Milestone, Washington, D.C." (2); and I also reference the Web site <-http://www.lonesailor.org/v12history.php>

CHAPTER 2: Do It Yourself
In this chapter, I reference or quote from L.S. Shoen's *You and Me* (12–13, 15–17, 20–21, 23); I also quote from an interview with Helen Shoen (1988).

CHAPTER 3: A.M. Carty and the Trailer Men
In this chapter, I reference or quote from David Halberstam's *The Fifties* (145, 160); L.S. Shoen's *You and Me* (10, 22, 30, 35–37); James Patterson's *Grand Expectations* (61, 66, 70–71, 73); notes from the Regular Meeting of the Board of Directors of the U-Haul Co. (November 3, 1948; February 2, 1949); notes from the Annual Meeting of the Stockholders of U-Haul Co. (January 20, 1951); and I also quote from an interview with Helen Shoen (1988).

CHAPTER 4: Go East
In this chapter, I reference or quote from L.S. Shoen's *You and Me* (29, 213); and *U-Haul News* (November 1954, 4).

CHAPTER 5: Slow and Steady Wins the Race
In this chapter, I reference or quote from David Halberstam's *The Fifties* (147–148, 488); L.S. Shoen, *You and Me* (29, 33); James Patterson's *Grand Expectations* (312); Pope John Paul XXIII's *Mater et Magistra* (17); and I also quote from an interview with Tom O'Donnell (1988, 9).

CHAPTER 6: Get in the Van
In this chapter, I reference or quote from *AMERCO World* (January 8, 1971, 12); David Halberstam's *The Fifties* (306); Jack Kerouac's *On the Road* (17); "How a Dealer Can and Will Do His Job" (10–11, 25); Richard Weingroff's article "Zero Milestone, Washington, D.C." (10); *U-Haul News* (November 1955, 1; April 1959, 9; November 1959, 10; November 1960, 27); and I also quote from interviews with Mike Morelli (1988, 4); and Jim Shaw (1988, 8).

CHAPTER 7: The Secrets of Success
In this chapter, I reference or quote from David Halberstam's *The Fifties* (500, 502); *U-Haul News* (August 1956, 1; October 1956, 1); "We're Asking for It" (1, 3–6); and I also quote from interviews with Mike Morelli (1988, 30); Tom O'Donnell (1988, 12); Jim Shaw (1988, 40–41); Helen Shoen (1988, 14); and Duane Swanson (1988, 3, 12–14).

CHAPTER 8: The Women of U-Haul
In this chapter, I reference or quote from Kahlil Gibran's *The Prophet* (29); James Patterson's *Grand Expectations* (34); *U-Haul News* (June/July 1963; September/October 1993, 18); and I also quote from interviews with Vivian Shaw (1988, 2–8); and Helen Shoen (1988, 12–16, 18).

CHAPTER 9: Taking the Lead
In this chapter, I reference or quote from Alan Brinkley's *The Unfinished Nation* (782); David Halberstam's *The Fifties* (117, 128, 132, 137); L.S. Shoen's *You and Me* (8); *U-Haul News* (December

1956, 2; October 1957, 1; June 1960, 11; September 1960, 6); and I also quote from interviews with Vin Kiley (1988, 17, 22–23); Tom O'Donnell (1988, 3–4, 6, 15–22); Jim Shaw (1988, 29, 32, 74); and Helen Shoen (31).

CHAPTER 10: To Be Reckoned With
In this chapter, I reference or quote from David Halberstam's *The Fifties* (243); and *U-Haul News* (July 1961, 3).

CHAPTER 11: E x KH = R
In this chapter, I reference or quote from L.S. Shoen's *You and Me* (118–119, 125, 127–128, 132, 135, 142, 147, 156, 158); "How a Dealer Can and Will Do His Job" (22); *U-Haul News* (November 19, 1959, 1); and I also quote from interviews with Tom O'Donnell (1988, 23, 29, 35–36); and Jim Shaw (1988, 54, 56).

CHAPTER 12: A Household Name
In this chapter, I reference or quote from David Halberstam's *The Fifties* (167, 170); James Patterson's *Grand Expectations* (499); L.S. Shoen's *You and Me* (32); *U-Haul News* (November 1959, 19; October 1963. 3); and I also quote from an interview with Vin Kiley (1988, 13).

EPILOGUE: This Day
In this chapter, I quote from Thomas Jefferson's "A View of the Rights of British America" (4); and quote from an interview with Helen Shoen (1988, 6–7).

INDEX